FROM LIBAU TO TSUSHIMA

FROM LIBAU TO TSUSHIMA

A NARRATIVE OF THE VOYAGE OF ADMIRAL
ROJDESTVENSKY'S FLEET TO EASTERN SEAS,
INCLUDING A DETAILED ACCOUNT OF THE
DOGGER BANK INCIDENT

BY THE LATE
EUGÈNE S. POLITOVSKY
*Engineer-in-Chief to the Squadron, who was killed at the
Battle of Tsushima*

TRANSLATED BY
MAJOR F. R. GODFREY, R.M.L.I.

The Naval & Military Press Ltd

Reproduced by kind permission of the Central Library,
Royal Military Academy, Sandhurst

Published by
The Naval & Military Press Ltd
Unit 10, Ridgewood Industrial Park,
Uckfield, East Sussex,
TN22 5QE England
Tel: +44 (0) 1825 749494
Fax: +44 (0) 1825 765701
www.naval-military-press.com
www.military-genealogy.com

© The Naval & Military Press Ltd 2010

The Naval & Military Press ...

...offer specialist books for the serious student of conflict. The range of titles stocked covers the whole spectrum of military history with titles on uniforms, battles, official histories, specialist works containing Medal Rolls and Casualties Lists, and numismatic titles for medal collectors and researchers.

The innovative approach they have to military bookselling and their commitment to publishing have made them Britain's leading independent military bookseller.

In reprinting in facsimile from the original, any imperfections are inevitably reproduced and the quality may fall short of modern type and cartographic standards.

TRANSLATOR'S PREFACE

No detailed account of the voyage of the Russian fleet to the Far East has to my knowledge been published. The newspapers occasionally mentioned it as being here or there, and of course its doings in the North Sea are a matter of history; but from the time it left Tangier until it met its doom at Tsushima it was practically in oblivion. By chance this book came into my hands, and I thought it would interest British readers.

Much has been said in derision of Admiral Rojdestvensky's fleet, but every one must agree that it was no mean undertaking to have brought this large fleet out to the Far East from Russia and laid it alongside the enemy. This was done, in spite of the difficulties of coaling without bases and of having to repair damages in the open sea. The fleet had to pass countries that were bound by the laws of neutrality, and some that were actually hostile to it. It was driven out of many ports by the ships of its allies. In spite of all these drawbacks, it accomplished a tremendous voyage with all "its units" intact.

That it failed to win the battle is in no way surprising. A great number of the ships were useless and obsolete. The crews were disheartened by the failures of their comrades at Port Arthur. The beginning of the movements which resulted in the open mutiny in the Black Sea and in the recent mutiny at Cronstadt were developing.

Finally, the spirit of the officers was not of the Nelsonian standard. We find the captain of the cruiser *Ural* flaunting his desire to surrender without striking a blow for his country.

It must be remembered that the dates are those of the Old Style, thirteen days behind those of the New Style, which has not been adopted by Russia.

PREFACE

EUGÈNE SIGISMONDOVITCH POLITOVSKY, engineer-constructor of the second deep sea fleet flagship, was born at Tashkend on November 12th, 1874. He received his education at the Emperor Nicholas I. Naval Engineering School, and left it in 1897. Up to the departure of the fleet for the East he served at the Admiralty at St. Petersburg. He went down in his ship, the battleship *Kniaz* (Prince) *Suvaroff*, in the fight of May 14th, 1905. This diary consists of extracts from his letters to his wife, which it must be understood were not intended for publication.

The diary is written entirely from the personal point of view of the author. He shares with the human being dearest to him everything that occupies or interests him. He writes in fragments, with detached sentences, sometimes snatching a few spare minutes from his duties for his letters. His diary is a full one. Scarce a day is omitted from the departure from Libau up to May 11th.

Involuntarily, one is impressed by the sincerity and justice of the author's tone. As he thought, so he wrote.

His style is very simple and graphic, despite its fragmentary nature.

The author was a constructor, not a sailor. This was his first cruise. His views of all that he saw are those of an independent person, bound by no traditions or clannishness. They appear to be absolutely impartial. In addition, through his position on the staff he knew much that remained unknown to others.

From the very beginning he did not believe in success for the Russian navy. The further the fleet went the more apparent did it become to him that it was going on a desperate and hopeless mission. "If you could but imagine what is going on," he writes—" if it were possible for me to tell you exactly all about it—you would be amazed. Should I live, I will tell you afterwards. No ! there is no use our fighting. Things have come to such a pass that I can only wring my hands and feel assured that no one can escape his fate, for this is the only possible assurance."

He took his duty very seriously and responsibly. Damages to the ships, and especially to the torpedo-boats, were constantly occurring, and it was necessary to repair them with self-improvised means under the most trying circumstances. For instance, can you not imagine the following scene ? A torpedo-boat in the open sea with a damaged rudder. Divers must be sent to repair it. The swell is tremendous, the boat is rolling fearfully, and around it are sharks. They lower the diver ; he is knocked about by the sea all the time—take care that he is not permanently disabled. They watch the sharks and drive them away with shots from a rifle. In spite of all these difficulties the repairs are completed.

Not one ship did the fleet leave behind, and this was in a great measure due to Politovsky. Whatever the weather, he tirelessly went from one ship to another, thinking out means of repair and accommodating himself to the most improbable and difficult circumstances, and always emerging from them with honour. Every one remembers his great work in getting the battleship *Apraxin* off the rocks at Gothland, where she had struck, icebound, in the winter of 1899.

With ships of the *Suvaroff* class he was well acquainted. From 1899 he was assistant-constructor of the *Borodino*, and this was probably the reason of his appointment to the fleet, an appointment destined to be fatal to him. How passionately he dreamed of the arrival at Vladivostok and of the possibility of returning to Russia! Alas! fate decided otherwise. He perished in his prime, being but thirty years old. Through his death our engineer-constructors have suffered a severe loss.

He was talented, clever, and energetic, with a vast experience gained from his cruise. What a valuable man he would have been in the construction of the new Russian fleet!

TABLE OF CONTENTS

CHAPTER I

BEGINNING THE VOYAGE

The Summons—The Emperor visits the Fleet—Worries and Work—Fear of Japanese Mines—Repairs—The Order of St. Anne—Mishaps—Suspicions and Nerve-strain—On the Dogger Bank—The *Kamchatka* " attacked "—The North Sea Trawlers—The *Aurora* fired on—The Ship's Barber—" Foggy Albion "—Crossing the Bay—Complications—At Vigo—Protests from England . 1

CHAPTER II

OFF NORTH-WEST AFRICA

Vigo and the Spanish—Chased—An English Escort—That Horrid Britannia !—A Memorial Service for Alexander III. — Cruisers — Tangier — Japanese Torpedo-boats at Hull—The *Suvaroff*—Morocco and the Moors—Rumours and Lies—Cutting the Cable—The *Malay* breaks down—Vessels in the Squadron—The Captain gets some Soap !—Great Heat—Dakar—Those English again !—Coal the Weakness — Sunstroke — Japanese Spies — The Natives—Visiting the Fleet—Heat and Thirst—Whales sighted—The *Malay* again—Strike of a Stoker 25

CHAPTER III

CROSSING THE LINE

Off Gaboon—Rats—Wiring for News—Requested to leave by the French—Cannibals—Awaking a King—Photographed with Royalty—A Captain reprimanded — Libreville — Dancing a Tam-tam — Andrew Andrewitch—Crossing the Line—How they fast—Great Fish Bay—A Portuguese Gunboat—Albatrosses—Dysentery—Angra Pequena—News of Mukden—English Possessions everywhere—German Sympathy—Sad News from the Front—Visiting the *Malay*—Lights put out—Rat Hunting 51

CHAPTER IV

ON THE WAY TO MADAGASCAR

Passing Capetown—A Steamer following—A Furious Gale—The *Malay* again in Trouble—Fire on the *Suvaroff*—Bad Coal—General Alarm—Another Storm—Madagascar in Sight—Sickening News from Port Arthur—Hopeless Darkness—The *Orel* invaded by Jews—A Swiss Schooner—St. Mary—Scenery and People—The French Cordial—Tangtang—Undecipherable Signals Japanese—Mysterious Signals—The *Esperanza* nervous—Port Arthur surrendered—Christmas—Warships sighted—Are they Japanese?—Mutiny on the *Roland*—Arrival at Nosi Be—The Admirals meet—Uncertainty and Dissatisfaction 79

CHAPTER V

AT MADAGASCAR

Life in a Torpedo-boat—Elephantiasis—Officers discharged—Sailors suffocated—A Funeral Service—

CONTENTS xiii

Further Tragical Mishaps—*Suvaroff* Shore Leave stopped—A Snake in the Hay—Requiem Service on Board the *Ural*—A Sad Spectacle—Population of Nosi Be—Frightened Oxen—Telegrams from Home—News of the *Oleg*—The *Kuban* arrives—Prickly Heat—Rumours of Return—Luxurious but Useless Ships—Animals on Board—On Shore—Gambling—Blessing the Water—The Rainy Season—The Mad Ensign—Intense Heat—*Malay* returns with Sick and Incapables—Arrest of Mutineers—The Foreign Legion—Pianola Musicians—Bad Meat—Shipping Cattle—Sinking of the *Bengal* Coal Steamer—Passive Resistance . . 108

CHAPTER VI

WAITING FOR ORDERS

Uncertainty—Firing Practice—Martial Law in Russia—Narrow Escape from a Collision—The *Suvaroff* flooded—Capture by the *Oleg*—On Shore—A Supposed Spy—German Methods—Playing for High Stakes—Our Hopeless Situation—Wasting Money—Man Overboard—Big Ships sighted—Internal Affairs in Russia—Rumours of Reinforcements—German Colliers—Confession under Difficulties—Europeans at Nosi Be—Breakdown of *Rezvy*—Complaints of Local Governor—Loss of Torpedo-boats—Shore Leave stopped—Apathy and Oblivion—A Narrow Escape—A Spy at Large—Sorting the Letters—Visit from Another Spy—Admiral Birilieff criticised—Waiting and wasting Time—A Sad Anniversary—A Comedy of Ladies—Money-changing—The Barber in Difficulties—A Humbugging Frenchman—Cleaning the Ships—Mysterious Balloon — Court-martial — Undisciplined Sailors—Rumours of Peace . . . 134

CHAPTER VII

EVENTS AT NOSI BE

A Nigger Wedding—Effects of Drink—Anxiety about the *Irtish*—Quarrels among the Officers—A Suppressed Telegram—Bad News of Vladivostok—A Dummy Dirk—Indignation at Home News—Good Work by Divers—The Malagassy impertinent—The Germans jeering—The General Staff anathematised—News about Mukden—A Prophecy—Examining the *Aurora*—Waiting for the *Regina*—Signal for Departure 167

CHAPTER VIII

ACROSS THE INDIAN OCEAN

Leaving Nosi Be—Confusion on the *Kamchatka*—Preparations—The *Regina* and the Japanese—A Grand Armada—Fearful Heat—Various Breakdowns—Steaming without Lights—A Star mistaken for a Ship—Cattle on Board—Chagos Archipelago—Artificer Krimmer—More Mishaps—Coaling at Sea—Look-out Boxes—Night Alarms—General Mismanagement—Success Unlikely—More Deaths—The Admiral's Weak Nerves—Guarding Divers from Sharks—Lights Ahead—Reflections on the Outlook—A Favourable Current—Opportunities of Attack—Life on Torpedo-boats—An "Iconoclast"—An Unjust Reprimand—Across the Equator—Japan's Advantages—Towing Torpedo-boats—Preparations for Fighting—Officers Drunk—Opium Cigarettes—Rats . . 183

CHAPTER IX

THROUGH THE STRAITS OF MALACCA

Mutiny—More Mishaps—Dogs—Straits of Malacca—Imaginary Torpedo-boats—Will the Japanese

CONTENTS

attack ?—Passing Malacca—No News of the War—Night Attack feared—Small Hope of Victory—Passing Anamba—Bound for Kamranh—Constant Fear of Japanese—A Time of Alarms—More Deaths 221

CHAPTER X

THE STAY AT KAMRANH

Arrival at Kamranh—Chances Neglected—Despair—Losing Time—More Accidents—Meeting of Admirals and Captains—Post Difficulties—A Goat—Cockroaches—Hard Work repairing—A French Cruiser—Food Scarce—Admiral Folkersham Ill—Meeting of Engineers—False News—A Regrettable Incident—Forest Fires—Foreign Contempt for Russia—Requested to leave Kamranh—Where is the Third Fleet ?—Two Colliers arrested—Fatal Errors—Discretion of the English Press—Phantom Submarine 238

CHAPTER XI

DELAYS AT VAN FONG

Sympathy of French Admiral—Japanese Spies—Expensive Food—The Russian System—A Rat Bite—Squalor—Want of Engineers—An Alarm—" Apes " and " Anyhows "—The *Oleg*—Preparations for Easter—Officers usually Drunk—Easter—Prickly Heat—Expecting Nebogatoff—Row on the *Orel*—Neutrality a Farce—Night Alarms—Buying Children—Suspicious Lights—No News of Nebogatoff—French Admiral as Poet—No News from Manchuria—Getting Cigarettes—The Annamese People—Nebogatoff in Sight—Excitement—A Good Post — French Impertinence — Poisonous Gases—Leaving Van Fong 263

CHAPTER XII

PREPARING FOR BATTLE

Expecting Torpedo and Submarine Attacks—Delay—Signals—Formosa—Coaling—A Steamer arrested—Love of Secrets—A Possible Japanese Scout—Contraband Ships—Preparations for Battle—An English Trick—A Balloon sighted—No Sign of the Japanese—The *Irtish* breaks down—Hopes of reaching Vladivostok 293

NOTE BY MADAME POLITOVSKY 306

APPENDIX.—OFFICIAL STATEMENT OF THE RUSSIAN LOSSES IN THE BATTLE 307

FROM LIBAU TO TSUSHIMA

CHAPTER I

BEGINNING THE VOYAGE

August 28th.—Events follow each other so fast that they get confused in the memory.

The return from the club in the morning, a frightened wife with a telegram, the rush from Petersburg to Cronstadt, hurried calls, appointment to the *Suvaroff*, good-byes, send-offs, a new service, etc., etc.

I am not yet accustomed to my new surroundings.

To-day I bade good-bye to the captain and officers of the *Borodino*, and to the foremen and workmen. They wished me good luck, drank my health, cheered, and the band played. They evidently had a very friendly disposition towards me.

The parting with the foremen and workmen was cordial. It was very sad to see their doleful faces.

They all cried before the end of their farewell speeches. I kissed all and thanked them. They blessed me with the ikon of St. Nicholas. I promised to give them my photograph as a memento. I had nothing else to repay them with. I could think of nothing better.

August 30th.—Yesterday we left Cronstadt. The Emperor overtook the fleet in the *Alexandria*, and steamed round it. All the time bands were playing, the men cheered, the fleet saluted. It was a superb sight. At times the smoke from the guns was so thick that the nearest ships were not visible. To-day we arrived at Revel at 7 a.m. It is said we are to remain here for nearly a month.

To-day is the *Suvaroff's* name-day. There was mass. No festivities.

8 p.m.—Such a worry. Nowhere can I find room for myself. When I was working on board the *Borodino*, as you may imagine, I constantly consoled myself with the thought of rest and of leave. The *Borodino* is completed. I might now have been free, might now have been living at home with my wife. But ah! fate! It seems to me that I shall not return. My predecessor in this cabin that I occupy went mad and was retired. This may be superstition, but it is nevertheless

unpleasant. It is said that to-day the captain of the *Asia* momentarily lost his head and steered his ship to ram the *Apraxin*; the presence of mind of the officer of the watch saved the *Asia* and *Apraxin* from damage.

October 3rd.—At sea, on the way to the island of Bornholm. Time flies. Daily there are new impressions, worries, gossip, and work. On the eve of our departure from Libau there was prayer, with genuflexions for " Boyarin Zenovie." [1]

Yesterday we had vespers, and to-day mass. Everything so triumphant and showy! The weather was glorious. At lunch the band played. Suddenly it was reported that the torpedo-boat *Buistry* (Rapid) had rammed the *Oslyabya*—had knocked a hole in herself and damaged her torpedo-tubes. The *Buistry* approached the *Suvaroff*. With the help of a megaphone (*i.e.* a large speaking-trumpet) the admiral conversed with her. They managed to plug the holes. It will be my work to mend them. We shall anchor off Bornholm, where I hope to repair the torpedo-boat. To-night there will be danger. We shall all sleep in our clothes and all guns will be loaded. We shall pass through

[1] Admiral Rojdestvensky's Christian name. "Boyarin" means "the lord."

a narrow strait. We are afraid of striking on Japanese mines in these waters. Perhaps there will be no mines; but considering that long ago Japanese officers went to Sweden and, it is said, swore to destroy our fleet, we must be on our guard. This strait is eminently suitable for torpedo-boat attacks or for laying down mines. When you get this letter we shall have passed the dangerous place, and it is no use your worrying yourself about it.

Have things gone badly with Kuropatkin again? How serious it is! Will there ever be an end to our reverses?

4 p.m.—We have passed the island of Bornholm without stopping. The southern shores of Sweden were visible. On the way we met a good many steamers. We are steaming with the greatest precaution. The fleet is split into several divisions, steaming at a certain distance from one another. Each division is surrounded by torpedo-boats. Whenever a steamer or sailing-ship is observed on our course or coming toward us, a torpedo-boat goes ahead and clears the way—that is, drives them aside.

It is a pretty sight—a torpedo-boat going full speed, gliding swiftly over the sea like a snake.

Being low in the water, it can scarcely be seen from afar.

October 4th.—At anchor off the coast of Denmark, opposite the island of Langeland (Longland). On board the transport *Kamchatka*.

Ah me, what a day it has been! We had scarcely arrived at Langeland when I went on board the torpedo-boat *Buistry*, not having even drunk my coffee. I put on high boots and took my mackintosh. The *Buistry* approached the *Kamchatka* and the work began. I got as black as the devil in the bunker. I must have new overalls. I shall buy some cloth somewhere and give it to a sailor to make.

High boots are invaluable, but it is a pity they do not come above the knee, as I sometimes have to crawl and spoil my trousers, just as I did to-day. The work in the *Buistry* is tremendous. The wind freshened. The torpedo-boat rolled. We should have worked outboard, but there was too much sea on; she rolled her deck under. The artificers will work all night at the inside, and perhaps to-morrow they may be able to do outside repairs. Towards the evening it blew so hard that it was useless thinking of getting on board the *Suvaroff*. It is very cramped in the torpedo-boat, and she is still rolling very heavily. I went over to the *Kamchatka*. I do not yet know if I shall get a cabin to sleep in. I brought very few cigarettes with me. Here, off Langeland, are a Danish cruiser and a torpedo-boat guarding our anchorage from the Japanese, who might fire a torpedo at us. There are Danish pilots in each ship, as well as in the torpedo-boats. Once we are out of the Baltic, the danger from mines will be passed.

I am sitting in the wardroom of the *Kamchatka*, where I have found some paper on which I am scribbling. If the weather does not abate I shall have to stay in the *Kamchatka* until we reach the next anchorage. They have just come to report that there are no spare hammocks. I shall have to spend the night on a sofa in the wardroom, without undressing. Well, that is no hardship!

I shall sleep somehow, as I am very tired.

October 15*th*, 12 noon.—At 9 a.m. I went from the *Buistry* to the *Suvaroff*. Find the consul is just leaving. I fastened my letter No. 3 somehow, unsigned, and gave it to the consul without a stamp. I think it will reach you.

At eleven o'clock I went to lunch with the admiral, who conferred on me the Order of St. Anne. This came as a surprise to me. The order with the ribbon was sent to me. The admiral is promoted to vice-admiral and aide-de-camp to the Czar.

3 p.m.—I lay down hoping to rest, but it was not to be; I had to go to the *Sissoi*—her davits had broken. They could not lower a single cutter. Off I went. Here we are at our first anchorage, and already there are a heap of damages. The *Buistry* is damaged; there are breakages in the *Sissoi*: in the *Jemchug* the davits broke and a cutter sank.

Three Danish steamers which coaled us are damaged. The owners assess the damages at 6,000 roubles (£600). I shall have to go and look at them.

I do not take into account minor mishaps, such as the torpedo-boat *Prozorlivy* (Clearsighted), which struck her bows somewhere, and of course bent them. She was, however, able to cope with the leak herself.

October 6th.—On the way to Cape Skaw.

Another mishap to the *Orel* (Eagle).[1] At a most critical moment, when we were going through a narrow strait, her rudder was injured. She anchored. The damage is not yet ascertained. There is probably some scoundrel on board who has

[1] On September 17th, 1904, the battleship *Orel* went aground when being towed to sea.

been trying all along to injure the ship. It is supposed to be one of the crew. We got up anchor at 7 a.m. The weather is fair, but it appears to be freshening. The wind is beginning to get much stronger, although the sun is still shining, and there is not much sea.

It is warm here, 12° to 13° R.

The *Orel* weighed anchor and followed the fleet.

October 7th.—We are not yet up to the Skaw. Shall be there soon. The weather is very fine again. I wonder what it will be like in the German Ocean. We have to put our watches back now.

It is 8.30 on board at this moment. In Petersburg it is probably not yet 8 o'clock.

I occasionally look at a book, *The English Self-teacher*, but I do not get on with it; sometimes I am lazy, and sometimes people interrupt me.

At anchor off the Skaw. There is no communication with the shore except through the pilot. I gave my letter No. 4 to him to post. Sending a telegram is out of the question. At present we have stopped at sea, and are not off a port. We were anxious about the *Orel* all night. As I have already told you, she left the fleet, no longer answered signals, and found herself in a dangerous place. Now she is anchored with the other ships.

I write to you so often now, that when it will be difficult to send letters, and they will take a long time reaching you, you are bound to be anxious. In any case, I warn you of this. Of course, I shall write to you as often as possible. I must finish this letter. The post goes very soon in the *Ermak*.

The next trip will be of some days' duration. We have no news of the war. It is very trying. The torpedo-boat *Prozorlivy* has damaged her condenser, and is being sent to Libau. The *Jemchug* lost a cutter and broke the davits. The davits were taken down to-day and sent to the *Kamchatka*, where, in hoisting them on board, they fell into the water and sank.

How strict discipline is now! A signal was made to the *Ermak*. She did not answer, so they began firing projectiles under her stern. After such a reminder she quickly responded.

At three o'clock a Swedish steamer approached the fleet, flying a signal that she had very important dispatches. Apparently the Russian agent reported that a very suspicious three-masted sailing ship had sailed from the fiords. An order has now been given to train all guns on every passing vessel. We met ships hitherto, but the torpedo-boats always drove them out of the way. We have already passed the most dangerous spots. Half an hour ago it was reported to the admiral that either the *Navarin* or the *Nachimoff* (I do not remember which) had signalled that they had seen two balloons. What can this be? Can it be the Japanese?

8 p.m.—Panic prevails on board. Every one examines the sea intently. The weather is glorious. It is warm. There is moonlight. The slightest suspicious-looking spot in the water is carefully watched. The guns are loaded. The crew are standing about on deck. One half will sleep at their guns without undressing; the other half and officers will keep watch to-night. It is curious that we are so far from the theatre of war and yet so much alarmed. The crew treat the matter seriously.

By the way, I will tell you the following incident. A sailor of the Revel half "equipage" asked to be allowed to go to the war in one of the ships. His request was refused. He thereupon climbed into the hold of one of the transports and remained there until now. Imagine how many days he passed in the fetid hold of the transport! Besides that, he would be suspected of being a deserter—that is, to have committed a severely punishable offence. No doubt they will inform Revel and keep him in the fleet. A curious incident, is it not? I wish the whole thing were over. Every one's nerves are strained just now. There are some officers in the fleet who have returned from Port Arthur, and they say that people out there are not nearly as nervous as they are in Russia.

The following details will show you how accustomed they have grown to the position. The crews of the ships at Port Arthur asked leave to go to the advanced positions, and returned under the influence of liquor. No one could understand how they became drunk. In the town liquors were not sold, and yet men went to the advanced positions and returned intoxicated. At last it was discovered, and how do you suppose? It appears that the sailors went to the front in order to kill one of the enemy and take away his brandy-flask. Just imagine such a thing. They risked their lives to get drunk! They did all this without thinking anything of it, and contrived to conceal it from the authorities.

October 8th.—The German Ocean (North Sea).

What a night it has been—nerve-racking and rest'ess. Early in the evening all were in a state of nervous tension and panic. News was received at midnight from the foremost ships that they had observed four suspicious torpedo-boats without lights. Vigilance was redoubled, but thank God the night passed happily. At present there is a fog. Nothing is visible all around. The sirens which you dislike so much are shrieking. I went to bed, dressed, last night, and did not cover myself with the counterpane, but just threw my overalls over me. In the night I froze, so covered my feet with a rug. The rug was very useful—many thanks to you for it.

We are now in the German Ocean. They say it will be rough. At present it is calm, but foggy. We go from the Skaw to Brest, in France. There, there will be no communication with the shore, it is said. It will be strange if we arrive in the East without having once set foot on dry land—and that seems likely to happen; circumnavigating the world and not seeing a single town—how that would please you!

9 p.m.—A signal has just been received (by wireless telegraphy) that the *Kamchatka*, which had dropped far astern, was attacked by torpedo-boats. Just off to find out details.

10 p.m.—The *Kamchatka* reports that she is attacked on all sides by eight torpedo-boats.

October 9th.—Night of October 9th.

The *Kamchatka* 's asking the position of the fleet. She says she has altered course and that the torpedo-boats have gone. On board us they think that the Japanese are asking the position of the fleet. The wind has freshened. The *Suvaroff* is rolling. If it continues to freshen, the torpedo-boats will be obliged to give up following and make for the nearest shore.

My God! what will the fleet do then?

About 1 a.m. they sounded off quarters, having seen ships ahead. They let the ships get nearer, and then there began . . . .

What it was words fail to describe! All the ships of our division were ablaze. The noise of the firing was incessant. The searchlights were turned on. I was on the after bridge, and was positively blinded and deafened by the firing. I put my hands to my ears and bolted below. The rest I watched from the spardeck, out of the accommodation-ladder port.

A small steamer was rolling helplessly on the sea. One funnel, a bridge, and the red and black paint on her side were clearly visible. I saw no one on deck—they had probably hidden themselves below in terror. First one, then another projectile from our ship struck this unfortunate steamer. I saw there was an explosion. The order to cease firing was given, but the other ships continued to fire and no doubt sank the steamer. A second and third steamer not having any one on deck rolled helplessly in the same fashion. The *Suvaroff* did not fire on them.

Imagine the feelings of the people in these ships! They were, no doubt, fishermen. Now there will be a universal scandal. As a matter of fact they are to blame themselves. They must have known our fleet was coming, and they must have known the Japanese wished to destroy it. They saw the fleet. Why did they not cut adrift their nets, if they had them out, and get out of the way? The nets could be paid for afterwards.

We shall find out at Brest what we have done. If it was not the *Kamchatka*, but the Japanese, who asked the position of the fleet, they will now know where we are to be found. If that is the case, we must expect to be attacked to-night. The moon is shining now, but from 4 to 6 a.m. it will be dark—the time most suitable for attack. If only we could get to the open sea! We shall be perfectly safe there from these accidents. I do not know whether to go to bed or not. You know I always like sharing even the smallest events with you and telling you of them. Take care of my letters; they are better than any diary. Perhaps some day I will read them myself and refresh my memory about our present excitements.

2.30 a.m.—What a misfortune! A signal has come from the *Aurora*, "Four underwater shot-holes, funnels torn, the chaplain severely wounded, and a captain of a gun slightly."

Our division fired on the *Aurora*. She and the *Dimitry Donskoi* were detached (we are in six divisions). At the time of the firing on the steamers the men lost their heads. Probably some one took her to be Japanese and fired on her with the six-inch guns; she was very far off. A very, very sad occurrence. The only consolation is that our shooting is so good.

3.30 p.m.—The second and third steamers about which I wrote last night suffered a little as well. The *Aurora's* chaplain had his hand torn off. They asked permission to call at the nearest port in order to send him to hospital. The admiral refused. Six different projectiles struck the *Aurora*, whose side and funnels were pierced. Comparatively few were injured. The *Aurora* is to blame for having shown herself on the horizon, on the side away from us.

She turned her searchlight on us, and by so doing made us take her to be one of the enemy's ships.

Yesterday, or more correctly this morning, I went to bed at six o'clock. Again I did not undress. I slept by snatches, on and off all day. Perhaps there will be no sleep again to-night.

The barber has just cut my hair. He uses huge tailor's scissors with cloth-covered handles. " I did not succeed in buying a proper pair," he explained, when he saw me looking at his ditty box.[1] He cut it very evenly for a self-taught barber.

Whom have we not among the sailors?—tailors, bootmakers, locksmiths, cooks, bakers, barbers, photographers, confectioners, cigarette makers, etc. All trades are represented, and there is work for all of them in a battleship. The captain wanted to be shaved, so he sent an orderly for a barber. The man arrived (not the one who cut my hair) and the shaving began. The barber's hand shook and the captain's face grew red with blood. He had nearly taken off half his cheek. A fearful row ensued. The captain, with soapy cheeks, smacked the heads of the orderly and barber. The latter

[1] A small wooden box in which sailors keep small articles of private property, such as watches, letters, photographs, etc.

tried to excuse himself by saying that he is still learning. A pretty picture, is it not? Now the captain shaves himself, not trusting local talent.

11 p.m.—An eventful day has gone by! At six o'clock some fishing-nets fouled the screws, but the engines are working. The fishermen in these parts tow very long nets, and you have to pass over them.

We had vespers to-day. How will this night pass? The weather remains fine. It is calm. The moon will shine until four o'clock. Perhaps another fog will come on like last night. All this morning the sirens were screeching in the fog. We shall be at the entrance of the English Channel in the morning. Again they have not served out hammocks to the crew. They will sleep at their guns fully dressed.

October 10*th* (7 p.m.).—In the English Channel, between England and France.

I have not written to you the whole day, and it is getting on my conscience.

We had mass in the morning, and then lunch. Not having slept all night, I lay down to rest. I slept until 3.30. I worked and then dined. I am only just free. The night passed quietly. It is raining now, and the ship is gently heaving on the ocean swell. If nothing further occurs, we shall be at Brest to-morrow. Passing by England this morning I saw her southern shores, which were faintly visible in the mist. Yes, there was "Foggy Albion." Involuntarily I pondered over this clod of earth—so powerful, so rich, so proud, and so ill-disposed towards us. We are only three hours' journey from London and six by rail from Paris.

Many varieties of birds settle on the ship, tired and exhausted by their long flight. The crew feed them and let them go.

I am depressed—fearfully depressed. Anxiety presses on my soul! What would I not give to be with you now! Again I have not slept all night. How tiring it all is!

October 11th.—They say it is very possible we shall not call at Brest. Profiting by the fine weather, we shall steer straight across the Bay of Biscay. The bay enjoys a bad reputation. It is seldom crossed in calm weather. It blows there very heavily. So far we have had a very fair voyage.

The *Korea*, which apparently called at Cherbourg, signals that she has heard nothing of the fleet having fired on steamers. The torpedo-boat *Bravy* has broken something.

Bay of Biscay.

STEAMING THROUGH MILK!

Fate herself prevented our going to Brest, and steered us straight across the Bay of Biscay to Vigo (Spain).

Such a thick fog came up at 1 p.m. that the ship astern was not visible. We are steaming through milk! The sirens are shrieking in turn, one ship after another.

The following ships are in our division: first the *Suvaroff*, next the *Alexander III.*, then the *Borodino*, *Orel*, and the transport *Anadir*.

Perhaps it is just as well we did not go to Brest. The entrance to the port is very difficult, dangerous, and impossible in a fog.

If we do not go to Crete, from Vigo onwards the way before us is wide—the whole ocean!

Lying on my bed last night I watched the rats making themselves at home in my cabin. I used to sleep with my feet towards the door, but have now put my pillow there, because of the rats. They can jump from the writing-table on to the settee, and could easily have jumped on my head.

Since we left the port of Alexander III. at Libau, a fortnight ago, no telegrams have been sent, except those allowed by the admiral. This was done so that spies should not warn the Japanese, waiting for us in the Baltic. The Japanese evidently thought (report said there were more than a hundred of them in the Baltic) that we should wait for the *Oleg* at Libau. The admiral, however, did not wait for the *Oleg*, and left. Their spies did not succeed in warning them. Though telegrams were received at the office, they were not sent on for two days. Perhaps this accounts for their inactivity.

Evening.—The fog dispersed and our division reassembled. The crew will sleep at their guns without undressing till we reach Vigo.

I sit in my cabin and try to distract my thoughts. Such gloom overwhelms me that I feel inclined to hang myself. I go into the wardroom, take a hand at dominoes, play with the dogs, or idle about, not knowing what to do with myself.

There are three dogs who are always to be found in the wardroom of the *Suvaroff*. One is a dachs called "Dinky"; the second a fox-terrier puppy, "Gipsy"; and the third, "Flagmansky," is something like a dachs, but white-haired and rough. Flagmansky and Gipsy are very amusing animals. They are often played with and teased; corks and papers are tied to them with string, and they jump and romp about. Now you know all our amusements. They are not many!

I go on deck and look at this much-vaunted sea.

Some one has prepared Flagmansky for the tropics by cutting off all the hair on his body, leaving his head like a lion's. The chaplain is accused of doing this, but he denies it.

We shall arrive at Vigo either to-night or to-morrow morning. It will be interesting to know if they will allow us to coal from our transport *Anadir.* Coal is getting scarce in the battleships.

October 12th.—We are approaching Spain. Lighthouses are already visible. We shall be at Vigo in the morning. We shall all be much relieved, as we have not called at a single port since we left Libau. We could go on to Tangier without stopping. The weather has greatly facilitated our passage.

Admiral Folkersham, commanding the 2nd division of battleships (in it are the *Sissoi, Oslyabya, Navarin, Nachimoff,* and another), distinguished himself when passing through the English Channel. He approached the English coast and coaled his ships from the transports. We are all laughing to think of the horror of our Minister for Foreign Affairs (by the way, all the ministers were opposed to the dispatch of the fleet, but the admiral insisted on it).

The Minister will be informed of the firing on the steamers. That will be the first European complication. They will then tell him about the coaling near England—a second complication. Finally he will learn that a whole division of our fleet has called at the neutral port of Vigo.

October 13th.—In Vigo Bay.

No communication with the shore allowed. I gave my letter No. 6, of thirty-two pages, to be forwarded by the Consulate. Of course, there were no stamps. I wonder if you will get it!

We shall not remain here more than twenty-four hours. The Spanish authorities do not allow a longer stay. This place is hot and sunny. There were 20° R. in the shade. The place is pretty. There are hills all around. The town is evidently not large.

12 o'clock.—The authorities do not allow us to stop for a moment. In order to gain time, the admiral asked the local captain of the port to telegraph to Madrid, to ask that we might stay here five days to make good defects. In spite of the prohibition we are about to take in coal, without which our fleet would be checkmated. Sentries will be posted over the hawsers (ropes which fasten the ships to the colliers), with orders to allow no one to cast them off. What will be the end of all this?

WILL THEY ALLOW US TO COAL?

A collier lies near each battleship, but they are not allowed to coal. Telegrams are sent everywhere. They are now waiting for a reply from Madrid. Will they really not allow us to coal!

The admiral has received a telegram stating that England is in a ferment—not at our having fired on the steamers, but because the torpedo-boat which was left on the scene of the drama gave no help to the sufferers. None of our torpedo-boats were there. They were at Cherbourg. The admiral replied to this effect to our ambassador in London.

An answer has been received from Madrid. It announces that the Government requests us to refrain from coaling, but will inform us to-morrow how much we may take.

The admiral ordered a signal to be hoisted for the fleet, to be in readiness to weigh anchor at 7 a.m.

When the admiral went ashore to-day, he was met in state. The crowd made an ovation, a description of which was in the local evening papers.

October 14th.—I gave my letter to a soldier or police "alguazil," as they call them on board. I gave him money—one peseta!

Our battleships lie waiting. It is positively insulting! Coal, bought by Russia, is in steamers close alongside and is not allowed to be put on board. "Who prevents it?" you ask. Miserable, beggarly, broken Spain. Undoubtedly the hand of England is visible in this. The Spaniards make no secret of it.

At 1 p.m. permission came for each ship to take in 400 tons. Sailors and officers, dirty and black, hasten to begin coaling. White tunics and cap-covers are nowhere to be seen. Everything is black with coal-dust. Faces are black as soot, and only teeth gleam white.

October 18th.—They say we leave for Tangier to-morrow morning. I have been busy all day, and not able to write.

CHAPTER II

OFF NORTH-WEST AFRICA

OCTOBER 19*th*.—On the way from Vigo to Tangier. Permission came last evening for us to proceed. At 7 a.m. to-day the fleet weighed anchor and left Vigo Bay.

I did not succeed in getting ashore. Yesterday an engineer of the *Anadir* fell from the upper deck into the hold, but escaped uninjured.

There is a report in the newspapers that, during the firing on the steamers in the German Ocean, the chaplain of the *Aurora* was wounded, and now they have sent him into hospital at Tangier, where the remainder of the fleet are lying. There is no proper harbour at Tangier—merely the open sea. It is unlike Vigo. The latter is one of the best harbours in the world. It is deep and long and broad. The Spaniards do not know how to profit by such natural wealth. Vigo might carry on a universal trade. At present it is a small provincial town on the sea. The Spaniards are very poor, because they are uncommonly lazy. Vigo trades mostly in sardines. They have a sardine factory. The sardines are caught in the bay, which is divided into squares for each party of fishermen. Heaven help the fishermen who trespass in the square of the others. There is a fight at once. This occurs so often, that there are special ships who part the fighters and tow the guilty fishermen in their boats to the shore, for punishment.

The weather is fine at present; but what darkness! Literally nothing can be seen, and there are no stars. Only lights that are absolutely necessary are left on deck. It is dark everywhere. One has to look out and not bump one's head or fall.

Something has gone wrong again with the *Orel's* steering engine. She continues to keep up with the others.

About 10 p.m. some ships chased us. They are now around us, and on the same course as ourselves. There are five or six of them. At one time it was completely dark, and then the ships behaved very defiantly—now extinguishing all their lights, now passing us, now chasing us, and now coming close up to us. Our division is steaming surrounded by them. They appear to be warships, judging by their shape, which we saw when one of them lighted up another with her searchlight. We are ordered to log all their manœuvres, lamp signals, place of meeting with them, etc. Hammocks are not served out to the crew, and they sleep at the guns.

The night has just become a little lighter. Stars have appeared, though sometimes clouded over. The stars and the Milky Way recall Tashkend to me. There, there are the same dark nights and bright stars.

It is supposed that the ships now surrounding us are English, and that at dawn they will disperse.

Hope we shall soon get to the ocean. There you can shape a course one hundred miles off, and no one will find you.

October 20th.—The English ships escorted us all night. They are now steaming on each side of us.

At eight o'clock the *Orel* hoisted a signal that her steering engine was damaged. All the ships stopped. The *Alexander* lowered a boat and sent the flag engineer to her. At nine o'clock our battleships and the *Anadir* proceeded to Tangier.

Sometimes the coasts of Portugal are visible.

When our ships stopped the English probably

took it for a hostile demonstration. They quickly assembled astern of our division and formed in battle order. Horrid folk! They are Russia's eternal enemy. They are cunning, powerful at sea, and insolent everywhere. All nations hate England, but it suits them to tolerate her. If you could only hear how furiously Spaniards abuse the English! They shake their fists and nearly foam at the mouth. If they only could, they would gladly play some low trick on them. How many impediments has this " Ruler of the Seas " put on our voyage? Every impediment has come from Britannia.

Do you know, we have passed by the shores of nine countries—Sweden, Norway, Denmark, Belgium, Holland, England, France, Germany, Spain. We are now passing by the tenth—Portugal.

Portugal is considered the ally of England, and upholds her everywhere.

Evening.—To-day there was a memorial service for the Emperor Alexander III. The English cruisers accompanied us all day, and at dusk again surrounded us in a semicircle. They are, however, steaming with lights, and are not playing any of the tricks they played last night.

If nothing happens we shall be at Tangier at

3 p.m. to-morrow. An hour ago we passed Cape St. Vincent (Portuguese), off which a great naval battle once took place.

It is beginning to be hot and stuffy in the cabins, although it is pouring with rain.

The number of English cruisers accompanying us has increased to ten. We are steaming completely surrounded by them. The ships are in this order :

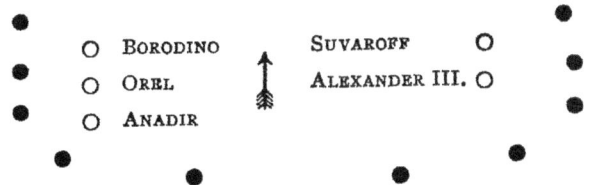

All this respectable company are going in the direction of the arrow. How small our division appears compared with the English! Will they escort us for long in this manner? Perhaps to Gibraltar, or perhaps even further! The crews again do not undress, and sleep at the guns. It is very trying for them.

There has just been a short mass and prayer. Three engineers, not yet having taken the oath, were sworn. The officers and men were fallen in on deck as on Sundays. The admiral made a short speech on the subject of the ten years' reign of the Czar, drank a toast, the crew cheered, and the band played. After that there was a grand lunch in the wardroom.

Morocco, in Tangier harbour.

The town of Tangier is unlike any we see in Europe. It is inhabited by Moors and Arabs. There are Europeans, but they live principally outside the town, which, with its white houses, is widely scattered over the hilly coast. From afar the town is beautiful. No one is allowed on shore.

You may remember once all the papers wrote that a Moorish robber had captured an American and demanded a ransom. This much-respected person lives twenty-five versts (nearly seventeen miles) from Tangier, and has built himself a costly villa with the money. It appears that he still occupies himself in robbery, and has a tribe of eight hundred men. No one is allowed to go far from the town.

We arrived here at three o'clock, and found all our fleet except the torpedo-boats at anchor. There are two French ships and an English one lying here as well.

At five o'clock the hospital-ship *Orel* arrived. She

is painted white with red crosses on her funnels. The Red Cross flag is flying at her masthead. The chaplain of the *Aurora* who was wounded on the 8th died from blood-poisoning.

There is a report that there are two Japanese torpedo-boats at Hull, in England. They are probably some of those who tried to attack our division.

It is rumoured that Russia has bought seven more cruisers, and that they will join us soon. This would be excellent. The battleships of our division are now coaling. There is frightful confusion on board. The sailors of the ship which coals quickest get a prize. The crew of the *Alexander III.* won 1,200 roubles (£120) at the last coaling.

Asusual, we have no news about the war! Yesterday was an anxious day for Port Arthur. The Japanese wished to hoist their flag there on the Mikado's birthday.

Scarcely had the *Suvaroff* anchored, when from all sides came steam cutters and boats with captains of ships, paymasters, and other officers. From the shore came the local authorities, our consul, contractors, captains of foreign ships—in a word, every one is hastening to the *Suvaroff* like the public to the play at the theatre! Truly it is like it! From our ship salutes constantly thunder, various flags are hoisted, and the band plays. From the other ships and from the shore they salute the *Suvaroff*. The scene is full of animation.

The native inhabitants dress very picturesquely, as though they were masquerading. Some are in jackets with wide breeches and a fez, and others in turbans and hooded tunics, all of various colours. The faces of all are very dark. They consider themselves of importance. It would be interesting to see them in the town.

Our torpedo-boats have already left for the Mediterranean. They have done this enormous journey in nineteen days.

10 p.m.—In the *Gibraltar Chronicle* they announce that Alexieff is leaving, and that Stössel has telegraphed that Port Arthur will be his grave.

October 22nd (night).—If you could only see what an inferno this coaling is! The steamers and battleships are lighted by electricity. The holds below and the decks are swarming with people. Words of command are abruptly given, and the band plays the gayest tunes. The work goes better to music. Though Morocco is considered under the protection of France, there is an English post-office, a German one, and I believe a Spanish one as well.

I have just returned from the steamer *Pallas*,

which brought coal for us and damaged her side while coaling.

A pedlar has just come on board, bringing picture postcards, mats, nets, white shoes and helmets (you know the kind the English wear in the tropics). I have already bought myself a helmet, and the postcards that are left are not much good, though I bought six of them and gave one to my servant. He is delighted. The boots do not fit, and white boots are an absolute necessity in the tropics.

Our consul's "cavass" has just come on board. He has a black face; wears a red fez, and a blue tunic with a hood; has bare legs and yellow heelless slippers. He is a curious object. He will stay with us till we leave, and will collect the mails. We shall have to pay a hundred francs for his boat. A modest sum!

Am just going on board the *Orel*. Something is damaged. . . . How wet I got! My legs were wet up to the knees. I went in the cutter to all the private coal-merchants, looking for the director of the company, and then on to the *Orel*. The rain is falling in bucketfuls, with such heaviness that it hides the other ships from view like a dense curtain. It is perfectly beastly. Luckily I have a mackintosh.

I have a trip to the steamer *Esperanza* before me. Hope I shall escape it.

7 p.m.—Went on board the *Esperanza*. Wore high boots, but there was no rain.

The local papers say that another of our ships has perished off Port Arthur. What is one to believe? For instance, there is a story in the papers that our admiral insulted the English admiral after the latter had tried to prevent our leaving Vigo. A quarrel ensued, guns were fired, and the English were beaten by us. They write so many lies in the local papers.

October 25th.—From Tangier to Dakar.

We left Tangier on the morning of the 23rd, and are now on our way to Dakar, which lies on the western shores of Africa, not far from St. Louis and Cape Verde, and belongs to France.

Have not written to you for a couple of days, for two reasons. I am very angry and very busy. I am angry because at Tangier I never received a wire from you in answer to mine. All day long yesterday, till the depths of the night, I was busy with sketches and calculations. I had not a spare moment.

When weighing anchor at Tangier the *Anadir's* anchor caught in the telegraph cable. By order of the admiral the cable was cut. I suppose there will again be diplomatic representations over this affair. No doubt the English will say that it was done purposely, so that no telegrams should be sent announcing our departure. It is lucky that the cable belongs to France. Had it been English the scandal would have been terrific.

At Tangier I saw a peculiar rainbow. It stretched from the foot to the summit of a hill.

7 p.m.—My work is accumulating tremendously. I began early in the morning, and probably will be busy again to-night with sketches and calculations. It will be a long time before you get this letter. As time goes on, letters will be less frequent. We have a tremendous journey before us—seventeen or eighteen days from port to port—so do not be anxious at not receiving news for a very long time. During our present cruise this is quite a normal state of affairs.

It is twenty-three days now since I set foot on shore. The shore is not attractive as a rule. I long to get quickly to Vladivostok. I am sick to death of it all. They say the sea is beautiful! I do not agree with that entirely. It is true the water is blue, but that is all you can say for it; it is only blue in calm weather, but in stormy weather it appears to me to be a stupid, insane, infuriated element. Perhaps the sea is beautiful, but only to those on dry land. I could never be fascinated by the sea.

October 26th.—The transport *Malay* broke some of her machinery at one o'clock last night. The whole fleet stopped and waited until she had made the defect good. We remained on the spot till 7 a.m. The *Malay* repaired engines and the fleet proceeded. We wasted six hours over it. I count every hour. The less time we spend in harbour and the quicker we go, the sooner we shall arrive at Vladivostok. In a word, Vladivostok is the goal of our desires.

October 27th.—We passed the Tropic of Cancer at 4 p.m., and are going towards the Equator. We are in the tropics, and yet I cannot say that it is specially hot and airless.

Our squadron going round Africa consists of the following ships: the battleships *Suvaroff, Alexander, Borodino, Orel, Oslyabya;* cruisers, *Dimitry Donskoi, Aurora, Nachimoff;* transports, *Kamchatka, Anadir, Meteor, Korea, Malay,* and the hospital-ship *Orel.* The *Meteor, Korea,* and *Malay* are under the merchant flag; and so is the *Orel,* but she is also flying the Red Cross.

We heard an unpleasant rumour to-day. It is said the squadron will make a long stay at Madagascar and carry out various exercises. Can it be so? This news annoys me. If we are there so long, when shall we get to Vladivostok? I console myself with the thought that this is a clever fiction.

The captain laid in a reserve of white soap, which dissolves in salt water (generally soap does not). The fresh water is preserved for steaming, so you can only have a salt-water bath on board. My servant brought me a piece of this soap yesterday. I do not know how he obtained it. There is nearly 100 roubles' worth of it on board the *Suvaroff*.

I have very few cigarettes left—only six boxes. It is a good thing you bought me 1,000 at Revel, and that I bought some at Libau, or I should be without them.

October 28th.—My servant is evidently attached to me. He is industrious and inquisitive. Just after we left Libau he saw a box of pastilles and said, "Did our barina [lady] really come to Libau, sir?" He came into my cabin to-day with a bucket and mop, and said, "Shall I interfere with your worship if I wash the deck?"

It is very probable that from Dakar we shall go to Gaboon. We shall call at ports which I have never heard of before, or if I have it was a very long time ago—perhaps at school.

I told the ship's photographer to prepare me a series of photographs which I will send you. They are not very characteristic, but better ones are not to be had.

October 29th.—It is very stuffy to-day. One perspires a good deal. Last night I slept with only a sheet over me, and had nothing on but a cross. Notwithstanding the stuffiness, one is obliged to sleep with closed ports and deadlights. In time of war all superfluous lights in a ship are either extinguished or covered over. If it is so hot here, it will positively be hell at the Equator. The air is offensive, being impregnated with steam. It is damp. The drawers of the tables are beginning to shut badly. They are sodden. Soon all metallic objects will begin to rust. I am sitting in my cabin with my shirt unbuttoned. Experienced people say that every one will get prickly heat. This eruption appears in the tropics because the pores of the skin are constantly irritated. The heat and stuffiness are unbearable. There is no wind—we are in a calm belt. The fans are kept going incessantly on board. Every one goes about sunburnt and sleepy.

AT DAKAR

Speed has purposely been lessened in order to get into Dakar to-morrow morning, and not this evening.

I think we shall stay in Dakar some days. Heavy coaling awaits us there—2,000 tons. All the decks will be loaded with coal.

Dakar, Senegambia.

October 30th.—Just arrived at Dakar. The fleet is anchoring.

The town is situated partly on shore and partly on a small island.

To-day is the admiral's names-day. They say there will be an official dinner.

The heat and stuffiness are fearful. Perspiration pours off one. The air is damp—towels will not dry.

2 p.m.—I have been on duty on board the cruiser *Admiral Nachimoff*. There I met an engineer whom I knew at school. I lunched in the *Nachimoff*, though there was an official lunch in the *Suvaroff*. I was not present. A sister of mercy from the *Orel* was there. She is a relation of the admiral's. The admiral has permitted communication with the shore after the coal has been taken on board. We remain here until the evening of November 3rd. All the ships except ours have begun to coal.

Negroes in small boats are rowing round the

fleet. You throw money into the water for them and they dive for it. The whole of their costume consists of a loin-cloth and not a stitch more. They are repulsive—black with long, thin legs and arms. They gave me the impression of being sick, incapable people.

Apparently, when the *Oslyabya* was at Tangier, she asked for a barge and baskets for coaling from Gibraltar. The English purposely employed all the barges themselves, and bought up all the baskets. The *Oslyabya* received nothing.

5 p.m.—The French Governor has just arrived in great state, and explained that he cannot permit us to coal. The admiral told him that he should, nevertheless, continue to coal until he had a telegram from Europe. They have long ago begun coaling in the other ships, and will soon begin in us. Perhaps the Governor will announce that we are not to remain here. That would be a great surprise to every one. Probably things are going badly in Manchuria—the French are evidently also sailing with the wind. From there (Manchuria) we have no decisive news.

Evening.—I hurried off my twenty-second letter to you as the post was going. It appears that telegraphing is very expensive from here. The cable between Dakar and Europe is damaged somewhere, so telegrams have to be sent round by America.

There is a report that Stössel is wounded in the leg. At first the French allowed us to coal, and then came an order from Paris not allowing us in harbour. Nevertheless, our fleet remains, and we are coaling. All the doors and scuttles are tightly closed to keep out the coal-dust. The stuffiness is dreadful inside the ship. We are tormented by thirst. Drinks are hot and unpleasant. All the same, one drinks incessantly. I alone drank six bottles of lemonade to-day.

Can you guess what our one topic of conversation in the fleet is about ? Coal ! It is our weak spot. Our comings, our goings, our voyage, and even our success depend on coal. In order to stimulate the men, they have established prizes, which are given to the crew of the ship that coals quickest.

The everlasting conversation about coaling drives one frantic, still one talks of it and quarrels about it.

October 31*st*.—Since early this morning I have been round the harbour. Coal-dust has penetrated everywhere—into the cabins, the cupboards, and on to the tables. The decks are clouded with dust. Every one is so black that you do not recognise people at once.

There is a report that we shall not call at Gaboon. Perhaps it is for the best, as we shall proceed sooner; besides, Gaboon lies almost on the Equator. That means it would be somewhat warm.

3 p.m.—They gave us ices for lunch to-day; they were steaming though cold. The heat is awful. Precautions are being taken against sunstrokes. There are some indications that we shall stay here till Wednesday—*i.e.* November 3rd. If we do not go to Gaboon, but steer for the next port on the list, we shall have a tremendous trip.

Our admiral called on the local commandant and invited him to lunch.

Just been urgently summoned on board the *Donskoi*.

November 1st.—Just returned from the transport *Malay*. She is damaged below the water-line.

Evening.—At 3 p.m. Lieutenant Nelidoff (son of our ambassador at Paris) died from sunstroke. The deceased was a wonderful linguist, knowing seven or eight languages. He will be buried to-morrow.

Our officers have just returned from the shore.

JAPANESE SPIES

According to them there is nothing interesting to be seen. If I can manage it, I shall go ashore tomorrow. I am too tired to-day.

November 2nd (5 p.m.)—I am sitting in a restaurant, drinking lemonade. How you would have laughed just now! I asked the negro waiter for the menu, and he brought me cards, dice, and a board covered with cloth. There is nothing to do on shore. I shall go on board by the first boat. They are burying Nelidoff. I hear the volleys.

I returned from the shore by the seven o'clock boat. Our doctor distinguished himself. He tore some fruit from a tree and ate it. Scarcely had he returned on board when he was seized with colic and vomiting.

There are some Japanese here. Our officers saw two of them. Evidently they are spies.

We leave to-morrow, and I go on board the *Donskoi* in the morning. I shall scarcely have time when I return to add two or three words to this letter before the post goes. Our trip will be a long one—about ten days.

I wandered about Dakar and thought of you all the time—with what curiosity you would regard all these unfamiliar pictures, the niggers, negresses, children, and lastly even the Europeans! Everything here is so original. Little children run about the streets without any signs of clothing. All the natives are bedecked with amulets. They are very lazy and obtrusive. One of them came to the captain and begged for money. The latter said to him, "Look here, you do nothing, so you have no money." The nigger fired back, "You have lots of money—do you do anything?"

There are few Europeans here, and very few elderly ones among them. After they have passed their youth here they leave the colony. The climate is said to be bad. An epidemic of yellow fever is raging. You may imagine that it is impossible to buy fruit.

The niggers to whom we threw coins into the water are already selling them, offering them back to the officers, as Russian money is not accepted here.

Many of the natives are rather picturesquely dressed in white and coloured tunics. The niggers go about with sunshades, but all are barelegged. The negresses sometimes wear European hats and garments something like dressing gowns. They carry their babies on their backs. Arabs are also to be met with here.

The religions are Catholic, Mohammedan, and idolatrous.

What a trade the town is doing since the fleet anchored! Many articles are doubled in value, and others cannot be obtained. The post-office is original. The clerks (niggers) sit in the building, and the public stand in the street and transact business with them through the windows.

November 3rd.—I have been all over the fleet this morning. I went on board the *Donskoi, Oslyabya, Alexander,* and *Borodino.* About 3 p.m. we weighed anchor. I do not know if we are going to Gaboon. There is news here that the storming of Port Arthur on October 20th was repulsed with heavy losses to the Japanese.

November 4th.—I went to bed early last night, leaving my port open. Early this morning, when they were scrubbing decks, water came in on to the table and sprinkled me a little. I jumped up and closed the port.

Last night they changed from one means of steering to another, for practice, in the *Suvaroff.* Something in her was not adjusted, and she very nearly rammed the *Orel.* Thank God all passed off successfully.

9 p.m.—The wardroom officers bought some birds at Dakar, but did not buy food for them. They

fed them with anything they could find, and now they are beginning to die.

Usually the band plays at lunch on holidays. To-day they suddenly began playing at dinner.

At meals we drink more than we eat. We suffer from dreadful thirst and drink pure water, mineral waters, red and white wine, beer, and different kinds of lemon juices. The admiral suffers most of all from the heat. During the coaling, when all doors and ports were closed, the temperature in his cabin reached 45° R. There are now 27° in my cabin, with the port open and the fans going which drive in the fresh air.

Some of the officers have bought themselves mats and sleep on them in the wardroom. The crew sleep on the upper deck.

Last night something happened to the engines of the transport *Malay*. All the fleet stopped and waited for her.

About 4 a.m. the *Donskoi* signalled that sand had got into her Kingston valves. That means the ship had passed a shallow spot, although the fleet was steaming 90 versts (sixty miles) from land. After the mishap to the *Donskoi* they went further out to sea.

It will doubtless be very hot to-day. Do you

know, the floor of my cabin is so hot that I can feel it through the soles of my boots.

7 p.m.—What awful heat! Again I have to keep the port closed, as the sea is splashing in.

One of the *Borodino's* engines is damaged. We stopped and waited for her. She is now steaming with one engine.

Storms are visible passing away from us in three places. The clouds are black and lightning flashes. It is close.

November 7th.—Something is wrong with the *Borodino.* The other engine does not work now. She gets hot bearings from time to time. We all stopped and waited for her. We are losing time over all these mishaps, and are losing it needlessly. The cruise of our fleet round Africa has no precedent in history.

Only by 8 a.m. did the *Borodino* put right her engines. The fleet is now pursuing its customary way.

7 p.m.—I saw two whales for the first time yesterday. There is nothing to look at except sea and sky.

Sometimes the men on watch collapse from the heat and have to be carried below. There are 61° R. at the top of the engine-room compartment, and we have not yet passed the hottest place.

They are preparing to celebrate the crossing of the line. The ceremony usually takes the form of a play given by the crew, and the immersion of all those who are crossing the line for the first time.

Twenty minutes ago something happened to our dynamo engine, and all the electric lights went out. The ship was steeped in absolute darkness. Now all is repaired.

My servant has just brought a white tunic and trousers, which he washed himself. They have turned out very well. "I don't think a washerwoman could have done it better," he said. "There is one drawback—they are not starched. But no matter; that's a trifle."

November 8th (11 p.m.).—As soon as ever night falls the same old story begins. From 8 p.m. until now the fleet stopped. We are only going at five knots. The unfortunate *Malay* has again delayed us. Something broke in her engine and the pump refused to work. I am very anxious about her. At Dakar she sprang a leak. I saw it, and reported that she could proceed without danger, working her pump. Just imagine it! The only pump she has is broken. She has nothing with which she can get rid of the water, and there are no docks near. At the present moment the *Roland* is towing the *Malay*, as one of her engines is broken and a blade of the screw of the other engine is broken off. Briefly, the *Malay* is unable to steam by herself. We are still far from Gaboon. Again there is a great delay. Thank God the sea is calm! If it were rough, the *Malay's* situation would be very dangerous. As it was, the *Roland* took a long time passing the tow-rope to her.

November 9th.—The *Roland* is still towing the *Malay*. As soon as they are able to coal her, she will be sent back. She will not then hinder and delay us.

When we were at lunch to-day they signalled to the admiral, saying that the *Kamchatka* had gone out of her course and signalled, "Dangerously damaged. Cannot proceed." Luckily, it turned out that the damage was trifling, and she was able to continue.

What a number of changes in climate we shall have had if we reach Vladivostok! We left Russia in very cold weather. Gradually it became hotter and hotter, till the heat was intense; then it will become cold again; then hot; and finally it will be very cold, as we shall reach Vladivostok in winter.

November 10th (night).—Again a bother with the *Borodino*. Something went wrong with her machinery. It was soon put right, but, nevertheless, time was lost over it. The *Malay* is still being towed.

Have found out about Gaboon. The fleet will not go within thirty versts of it.

All communications with Gaboon will be *viâ* the *Roland*. Of course, no one will be allowed to land, and we shall all kick our heels on board. Our ships cannot go nearer, owing to shallows and banks.

The *Meteor* signalled to-day that one of her stokers has struck work and refuses to keep up the necessary amount of steam. The captain asked to be allowed to deal with him himself. The crew of the *Meteor* are volunteers.

I have been sitting all day long over plans and calculations. The scuttles were open, and now and then waves came splashing over my table. I went to the ship's ice-chamber, and it seemed cold to me after the heat which reigns everywhere.

The day passed strangely. I hardly went out of my cabin, and got through a lot of work. I must go and air myself, as my head has grown heavy.

CHAPTER III

CROSSING THE LINE

November 13*th* (10 p.m.).—*Off Gaboon.*

This is how it has all turned out! We stopped this morning and anchored. No one knows where we are or where Gaboon lies. We have sent the *Roland* north to the coast to find a lighthouse and Gaboon. We see land, but the place is unknown.

I caught a glimpse of a shark. When we were weighing anchor at Dakar, a cutter approached with some important documents (perhaps it was the post). In the hurry of departure the papers were not taken on board.

The navigators, including the flagship's navigator, were confused. It proved that we were thirty miles (fifty versts) below Gaboon. We are now going back to Gaboon, and we shall have already twice crossed the Equator. The celebrations only take place at the first crossing. When we strike the Cape of Good Hope we shall have crossed it a third time.

6 p.m.—We are anchored. A French boat has just arrived bringing some dispatches. In coming the boat was nearly stove in, as it caught in our wake. Luckily it escaped, and only the rudder was broken.

The rats are making themselves felt. Three nights ago a rat bit the first lieutenant in the foot, and last night gnawed off one of his corns. What do you think of that?

The French officer dined with the admiral. He does not know what is going on at the war. Even the telegraphic agencies' telegrams are not received at Gaboon. A fine town this! And there are many like it in the colony. I don't think we should find a town like it in Russia. Not even the governor of this place gets telegrams. There are only about seven hundred Europeans here; the rest are negroes, amongst whom are cannibals. During the last two months the cannibals have eaten two Europeans.

They say that an English steamer will arrive tomorrow, bringing us newspapers of October 27th (Old Style). On the 16th or 17th the steamer will go back to Europe, taking our mails.

As we have no news from the war, the wardroom officers of the *Suvaroff* have asked the admiral permission to send a prepaid telegram to the *Novoe*

Vremya, asking for news. The admiral refused the request, but will wire to Admiral Wirenius, who will send us the latest intelligence from the Far East.

The admiral has received a telegram from Petersburg advising him not to stop at Gaboon, but go to some other place, as the French wish our fleet to leave this port. They point out a more convenient bay, and promise to give us pilots. Nevertheless, our fleet will stay here as long as necessary.

What was the end of the shooting affair in the German Ocean, near Hull?

They say the astonishment of the local Europeans is very great. First one steamer arrived "for provisions," then a second, then a third, and finally our fleet. No one ever expected that we should call at Gaboon. It is just as well, perhaps. The more our movements are known, the more unfavourable orders we might have from the French Government.

November 14th (11 a.m.).—Have already been on board the *Orel* and *Alexander*. At two o'clock shall go on board the *Nachimoff, Borodino,* and *Meteor,* which are badly damaged and leak.

The Governor has sent us a present of fruit and vegetables. At lunch we had pineapples, bananas, mangoes, and something else. Pineapples are the nicest.

On board the *Alexander* they accidentally carried off a negro from Dakar, whom they have landed. He says the negroes here eat their dead, as cattle are scarce and meat is dear. Before they eat them they cut off the hands and feet and put them in a bog to swell. The flesh is then more tender and tasty.

They do not risk sending divers down here, as there are too many sharks.

The Governor sent some other fruits besides. No one knows what they are—either grass or vegetables. They have received a telegram in the private transports saying that Kuropatkin has driven the Japanese back to the coast. That would be good news, but it is difficult to believe.

11 p.m.—The vegetation here is very rich, judging by the reports of those who have been ashore. A "regular botanical garden." A moth flew on board—such a size, I am afraid you will not believe me, but it was nearly a foot! We saw a turtle in the sea, 2½ feet long. The Frenchmen on shore showed us a dead boa-constrictor 18 feet long.

The officers who went ashore called on the king of the place. He was asleep. They woke him without ceremony, looked at him and his wife, and went away. He is just a wild nigger, like his subjects.

I told you about the vegetables the Governor sent us. We tipped the man who brought them a pound sterling. He seemed much confused, accepted the money, and then did not know what to do with it. I think he will spend it on our wounded.

November 15th.—They say there was a very violent storm last night. I heard nothing, and slept through it all.

The officers have returned from Libreville, where they went at nine this morning. They relate many interesting things, and are in rapture over the vegetation. They have brought some fruit and a couple of parrots. They bought one of the parrots for ten francs, and the other was sent to the admiral by a Jesuit father with the fruit, as a gift.

The same man who was given the pound, out of kindness acted as guide to the officers. When taking leave he feared a repetition of the tip, and kept on repeating that " he wanted nothing."

The officers paid another visit to the king. He received them in an English naval uniform and cocked hat. They were photographed with him and his wives. One of them was taken arm-in-arm with the queen-dowager, who begged for money. Some of the court ladies were drunk. It is two days since the king, who is seventy-two, succeeded his brother on the throne. Margarita, the eldest lady-in-waiting and a most energetic old negress, runs about naked. For that matter, the inhabitants in general do not trouble about completeness of costume. The natives respectfully greet all Europeans. It is a curious monarchy, under the protection of France; more truly it is her colony.

To-morrow there will be something in the nature of a coronation on shore. The dead king is at present lying in a box under lock and key. One of the officers sat on this box, to the consternation of the present king and his court minister. The latter was dressed in a cocked hat, a necktie round his bare neck, cuffs, sword, and frock-coat, but without linen or trousers—a beautiful figure, thus attired, at the reception of the guests.

November 15th.—You can imagine what sort of a town is Libreville. The Governor sent the admiral the latest news from the papers. They are dated October 2nd—the day of our departure from Libau.

November 16th.—I did not succeed in finishing my last letter, as the boat left for the shore. In it went the last post which can go by the steamer leaving for Europe to-morrow morning.

From sunset to dawn the admiral has forbidden communication between the ships and the shore. Yesterday at 10 p.m. a cutter from the *Donskoi*, in the harbour without special leave from the admiral, was detained. The officer of the watch was put under arrest for this for three days. This evening a boat from the same ship with three officers, also in the harbour without special leave from the admiral, was likewise detained. In to-day's orders the captain of the *Donskoi* is reprimanded, and the three officers who were in the boat are to be tried. They are to be dismissed to the steamer leaving here for Europe to-morrow and will go to Russia. As you see, disobedience is severely punished on board.

9 p.m.—To-day a sub-lieutenant of the *Alexander* told me about the negro whom they took from Dakar. When his boat shoved off from the *Alexander* he began to storm, shout threats and curses at the boatmen, stamp on the deck with his bare feet, etc. When he saw that he could not get away from the *Alexander* he sat on the turret and wept burning tears. The crew surrounded him and looked on, laughing at this healthy, bellowing lad. Seeing that there was

nothing to be done, he grew resigned. It appeared he was very jealous and uneasy about his wife. Very soon the crew made friends with him, and taught him several Russian words. His memory was phenomenal; in a few days he learnt the names of nearly half the crew. The soles of his feet seemed very funny to the sailors. They are half white, as they are in all negroes. On the trip the officers collected 60 roubles for him. He left exceedingly satisfied. He serves in a shop, and, being rather civilised, speaks French fluently.

November 17th (7 p.m.).—Half an hour ago I returned from the shore, where I had gone in the *Roland*.

We reached Libreville at 8 a.m. About ten we reached the town, if this settlement can be so called. We could not approach close to it in the *Roland*, so got into boats. I went with the officers of the *Borodino*, and was with them all the time. First we went to a restaurant for refreshment. There were six of us. They gave us three bottles of lemonade, a little bread, fish, meat, peas, cheese, and fruit, and charged fifty-five francs. We left the restaurant and went along an avenue of palm-trees. We went to a German factory, to the Catholic Church, to two or three little villages, and to the plantations. There was not much time, and we turned back. We called on the king, then went to a shop, then to the quay and back to the *Roland*. Although I was only five hours ashore, I was fairly tired, probably from not being accustomed to exercise. Several photographs of our party were taken. We were taken with the negroes serving in the French army, with negresses in the villages, in the plantation, and in the King's ground under a tree with a small negress who ran after us.

The king came out and placed a chair for each of us, and sat down in an armchair on the terrace. He and all his courtiers were dressed. A nigger all covered with grass and with a semblance of a mask over his face (not the slightest bit of his body could be seen) danced a Tam-tam, accompanied by savage music. Our time was short. We rose, and the king shook hands with us all. By this time many officers had gathered at his palace. They wandered into all the corners of his house. The dowager-queen sat in a hammock drunk, and tearfully begged for money. While rambling through the plantations I bought a lot of pineapples, bananas, and cocoa-nuts.

The plantation where we sat eating fruit belongs to a Frenchwoman, a native of this place. We thought her house was a restaurant, and unceremoniously demanded lemonade, water, etc. It then appeared that it was a private dwelling. The Frenchwoman was very friendly—told us about herself and her children, who were being educated in France. She sent two negroes to carry our purchases to the pier.

How rich the vegetation is in this place! You seem to be walking in a botanical garden. All around are palms, bananas, lemons, mimosa, lianas, mangoes, baobabs, and wonderful flowers. The trees are immense and lofty.

On our return we called at a shop for drink. They gave us cider. If you had been here, what would you not have bought! We purchased all sorts of rubbish—negro instruments, teeth of wild animals, poisoned spears, weapons, etc. In the town we met the negro who was brought by the *Alexander*. He now answers to the name of " Andrew Andrewitch," which was given him by the crew.

November 18th.—I woke early this morning. I had a trip to make to the private transports.

5 p.m.—Leaving Gaboon.

About an hour ago we weighed anchor. Our destination is unknown.

To-day on board the *Alexander,* which is astern

of the *Suvaroff*, they celebrated the crossing of the line. We could see how they capered and splashed water about. In the *Orel* something has happened to the electrical steering gear, but she is steaming and does not detain the fleet.

November 19*th*.—At 9 a.m. we began to celebrate crossing the line on board. Neptune, Venus, a navigator, sub-lieutenants, Russian peasant-women, devils, barbers, and tritons arrived on field gun-carriages drawn by black naked people. All this fine company came from the stern of the ship, accompanied by buglers and to the sound of a march, played by the band, which was stationed forward. They approached the fore-turret and climbed on to it. The audience took up their places in the bows, on the bridges, turrets, masts, yards, and crosstrees. The admiral, captain, and officers stood on the bridge. The actors were all half naked, and were painted in the most varied colours—black, green, red, yellow, blue, etc. Neptune had his trident and a great beard of tow. The navigator had a chronometer, binoculars, and a sextant. The peasant-woman had a baby, which was represented by the fox-terrier. When the baby was supposed to cry, they twisted the dog's tail to make him howl.

The actors played well. Near the turret was a huge bath, made of canvas and filled with water. When the play was over, they turned the hose on to every one, from the admiral down to the sailors. The actors were first thrown into the bath, and then the rest of the ship's company. After being ducked, their faces were lathered with a huge brush dipped in whiting, and they were shaved with a very large razor (two and a half feet long), made very cleverly from a piece of wood. The water in the bath was clean at the beginning, but after the actors who were painted had been ducked, it turned into God knows what colour. Nearly all the officers, the captain, and the flag-captain were ducked and shaved. I and several others escaped the bath; nevertheless, I had not a dry spot on me. Any one who hid was hunted out and ducked. The messman shut himself up in his cabin. They could not get at him, so they removed the deck-plate above it and poured water in. The messman at last, to save his things, came out and was thrown into the bath. Even the chaplain did not escape the same fate. It was a good thing for those who fell in feet foremost. When it happened the other way, their heads were pushed under and their legs held up. One of the dogs who was thrown into the water climbed out on to the nearest bitts,

GOING TO GREAT FISH BAY

and looking at the people struggling near him, raised a deafening howl.

The crew evidently enjoyed their holiday. It was a great diversion for them, as they had not been ashore since we left Revel.

About four o'clock something went wrong in the *Malay*. An officer was sent to replace the captain. All the fleet stopped for the transfer of the officer from the *Suvaroff* to the *Malay*.

The fleet is now going to Great Fish Bay, which belongs to Portugal. If for any reason we cannot call there, we shall steer for Angra Pequena (under the protection of Germany).

November 20th (7 p.m.).—We had vespers on board. The service pleases me, especially in the ship. Though around one are only the faces of officers and men all dressed in white, and though the acolytes and choir are barefooted, the chants and intoning remind me of dear, far-distant Russia.

November 21st.—It is beginning to be less hot. The greatest heat, or more correctly closeness, was at Dakar. Now it is fairly tolerable. When we reach the Cape of Good Hope we shall have to put on ordinary uniform, and perhaps greatcoats. They say it will be very hot and damp in the Indian Ocean.

All the crews in the fleet have begun to fast, by order of the admiral. Do you know how they fast? They eat their food as usual, only they go to church.

If the reckonings are correct, and all goes smoothly, then by the end of January or the beginning of February our fleet will be near the shores of Japan. This will mean that there will be only about two months more of the wearisome, monotonous life which we are all leading. It will not be long before we join the ships that went by the other way. Much depends on the position of the Port Arthur and Vladivostok fleets, as well as of Port Arthur and Vladivostok themselves. It also depends on how matters stand with Kuropatkin at the time of our arrival in the East.

Judging by descriptions, Great Fish Bay is not an important place. The settlement consists of seven houses, two of which are uninhabited. It is surrounded by the desert. There is no water, so it has to be brought from a distance. Fish are plentiful. It is a very good anchorage. We shall probably be there to-morrow morning.

It is cooler now. In my cabin there are 24° R. The drawers of the table can be pulled out once more.

November 23rd.—The temperature continues to

fall. In the open at present there are only 14° R. They count on arriving at the anchorage at twelve o'clock. We are now going further from Port Arthur, but after doubling the Cape shall approach it. The voyage from Tangier to Port Arthur is about the same as the voyage from the Cape to Port Arthur. What a much longer distance we have come by going round Africa!

1.50 p.m.—We have arrived at Great Fish Bay. It is not particularly pretty. On one side the shore is high and jagged, and on the other it is flat. There are small houses in several places on the low-lying shore. From the ship they can hardly be seen, even with a telescope. The shore is sandy. No doubt there is neither post nor telegraph station here. Wherever one looks there is sand—nothing but sand.

A Portuguese gunboat has just passed the *Suvaroff*. (Her name is *Limpopo*.) She is a very small and insignificant ship. She was anchored far out in the bay, and has now gone no doubt to acquaint the authorities that our fleet has arrived and anchored at Great Fish Bay.

This will be a surprise for the Portuguese. We do not, however, stay here for long. To-morrow evening we get up anchor.

4 p.m.—It appears that the Portuguese gunboat, *Limpopo*, went round the fleet and stopped near the *Suvaroff*. Her captain came to the admiral with explanations. I do not yet know what he said, but it can be nothing pleasant for us. Yesterday, before the fleet arrived, the gunboat compelled one of our colliers to put to sea under a threat of firing on her. The moment the fleet arrived the colliers re-occupied the places assigned them by the admiral. They say the admiral assured the commander of the Portuguese gunboat—or, more correctly, led him to suppose—that the fleet was four miles from the shore; that is, that it was in neutral waters.

Amongst other things, the Portuguese stated that it was known that our ships would call at Great Fish Bay. Curious how this could have been known at Lisbon, where the arrangement to send a man-of-war here was made. Probably they were informed by the English, who jealously watch every movement of our fleet. The hospital-ship *Orel* has left, and will call at Capetown.

We shall go to Angra Pequena from here. The Germans (to whom it belongs) call it Lubevitz Bay. It is situated one thousand versts from here. We leave this to-morrow at two o'clock.

November 23rd.—At anchor in Great Fish Bay. An hour ago I gave my letter to you to be sent to Europe by one of the steamers that is returning. The captains of the steamers had been on shore. They say that the beach is strewn with lovely shells and crowded with red flamingoes. The captain of the Portuguese gunboat told the captains of the colliers that he would forbid any attempt on their part to coal the fleet. What naïveté—or rather, what impudence!

I have ordered them to call me at 6 a.m. to-morrow, in order to go to several ships.

November 24th.—From Great Fish Bay to Angra Pequena. I could not sit down and write to you all day. Somehow, everything went wrong. Just as I seated myself I was called away. I was on board the *Borodino* to-day. I saw some Libreville photographs. They are very small; you cannot make out the faces.

At four o'clock all our fleet began to weigh anchor. Two hours later the *Malay* hoisted a signal that something had happened to her rudder. The *Roland* was ordered to take her in tow. The hospital-ship *Orel* is also going with us. Whales and albatrosses are seen more and more frequently. The albatrosses fly a tremendous distance from the land, and are very large; sometimes they measure sixteen to seventeen feet across the wings.

Life on board is monotonous. One day is like another. You live in the past (at all events, I do), and dream of the future.

November 27th.—We passed the Tropic of Capricorn to-day. We are approaching Angra Pequena. We have lessened speed, in order to get there in the morning. The flagship's navigator considers that half our voyage will have been completed when we reach the southern end of Madagascar.

At Angra Pequena I think we shall get news from the East. The Germans are probably more interested in the war than the French.

A sailor in the transport *Korea* has been seized with dysentery or malaria. God grant that the disease does not spread. Hygienic conditions are disregarded in the fleet. Many go on the sick-list. The wind has risen, the waves have increased. Before entering Angra Pequena boats will be lowered and will take soundings. The place is little known. Some ships might go aground. The post has already been collected. I hope to be able to send this letter to-morrow morning.

November 28th.—Approaching Angra Pequena. We have not yet reached the anchorage. We are steaming very slowly, for fear of going aground. The wind is still increasing, and the waves are dashing over the poop (the after-part of the upper deck). Even if the weather gets no worse our cruise round the Cape will not be a very happy one.

At anchor at Angra Pequena.

About one o'clock we reached Angra Pequena. The battleships anchored, but the cruisers remained at sea. There is not much room in the bay. It is impossible to stand on deck in unsheltered places. It blows fearfully. The waves are washing over everywhere. No boats have been lowered yet. There is no communication with the shore, or even between ships. The post has not been sent. You may imagine what the strength of the wind is when it is estimated at a force of ten.

Report says that the mail-boats call here five times a year. Possibly one of the colliers will be discharged, and return to Europe from here. In that case the mail will be sent in her.

November 29th.—The wind abated a little during the night. A steamer came alongside, but the sea was so high that her side was crushed. One of our 75-millimetre guns was damaged, and a port was broken, which will have to be repaired or changed. Spare guns are carried in the transport.

This is the third day that the mail-boat has been detained owing to the weather. We hear, from English sources, that there has been a fight at Mukden; the losses on both sides amount to 50,000 men. It is also said that the Japanese have taken by storm one of the forts at Port Arthur. The Russians blew up this fort, and 30,000 Japanese perished. All this is hearsay

On shore they say that a certain steamer puts to sea every night and watches passing vessels. Evidently this steamer is freighted by the Japanese, to follow and perhaps strike a blow at our fleet.

Men are going out of their minds in the fleet. An ensign of the reserve serving in the battleship *Orel* went mad, and also a sailor in the transport *Korea*.

An English steamer arrived here and left at once. A German transport arrived with troops to put down the native rising in the interior. The mail apparently was not sent, and the mail-boat has already left. Perhaps they will be able to send it by the troopship, which is probably returning to Europe. Everything, as you see, is uncertain. We stop on and on here for no reason. It is still blowing hard. There is no communication between ships, and I ought to go on board the *Malay*.

November 30th.—We remain at anchor.

Every precaution is taken. Searchlights illumine the horizon.

Close to the fleet are two small islands belonging to England. It is perfectly astounding—wherever you look on the map there are English possessions, although they are small. Angra Pequena formerly belonged to England. She ceded it to Germany, but the two islands remained in her possession.

Wherever we have called, the local authorities (some, perhaps, only outwardly) placed impediments in the way of our fleet. Angra Pequena is the first German port at which we have called, and the authorities are very friendly.

The local commandant says that "he is not a diplomat, and he does not know officially of the arrival of the Russian ships. They are anchored behind a bend, and are not visible from his windows."

I forget that Denmark also put no obstacles in our way; but, judging by the tales of those who have been in Denmark, the Danish people sympathise with Japan, and not with us. The Government involuntarily helps Russia. It is quite different with Germany. The sympathy of both people and Government is on our side. I do not know how it will be later, but at present we have nothing to reproach the Germans with.

We do not know when our stay here will end. An English (Capetown) newspaper has been brought on board. Sad news! Kuropatkin has not moved, and according to the paper he received a reinforcement of 34,000 men after the battle of Liao-Yang. Can it really have been so few? The commander of the second army has only just arrived at Harbin—which means that the army is not yet in being. We learn that Kaulbars is appointed commander of the third army; he is said to be a very incapable general. At Port Arthur the Japanese have taken a hill that commands all the harbour. The ships are at a disadvantage, and they are hurriedly preparing to go to sea. This is the news imparted by an English paper. How sad it all is!

Officers who have been to the post-office on shore found out that only ten Europeans—Germans—live in the settlement. They saw the troops sent out from Europe by Germany to subdue the natives. There are 1,200 men. Two of the German officers speak Russian, one of them excellently. There is general hatred of England here as well. She supplies with arms the natives whom the Germans are now going to subdue. She is evidently a country that tries to damage every one and to work mischief everywhere.

The wind is still howling. We are waiting for it to go down. At our anchorage there is mishap after mishap. The *Malay* and the *Meteor* have just signalled that their engines are so badly damaged that they cannot repair them without help. The co-operation of the *Kamchatka* is necessary, but I could not go on board.

December 1st.—Yesterday from 10 p.m. to 1 a.m. I was going from one ship to another in a steam-cutter. What a time I had! The cutter pitched and rolled violently. She dipped her bows under and shipped large quantities of water. It was difficult to see because the salt spray blinded one. Sometimes the cutter pitched so much that her screw was out of the water and raced. To complete our discomfort, it was quite dark.

After I had been to several ships I had to go to the *Kamchatka*. We could not discover where she was in the darkness. We searched for her. She was lying further from the shore than the other ships. It is difficult to describe what it was like near her. It seemed impossible not only to go on board her, but also to receive a bag which was lowered over her side. I had on a mackintosh, but there was not a dry spot on me. How was I to get on board? It was pure torture. It was impossible to go alongside the ship without the risk of breaking up the cutter, which was absolutely prancing on the water. There was no accommodation-ladder, so we had to get up by a rope-ladder, choosing a favourable moment. God help you if hand or foot slipped. You would either fall between the ship and the cutter and be crushed, or be struck by the screw if it were moving, or run the risk of falling into the jaws of a shark. Yesterday an officer fell like this, but luckily escaped with only a ducking. I again ran the risk of falling into the sea when going on board the *Malay*. I had only just seized hold of a rope when the cutter was torn from under my feet. I hung over the water, but got on board somehow. I shall not forget yesterday in a hurry.

To-day it is nearly calm.

Calm! I had to go to the steamer *Ratzentaler*; she was damaged. I reached her safely and examined her. This took me about an hour. I came up from below to get into the boat, and this " thing " called the sea was as boisterous as ever. With difficulty I let myself down into the cutter. She rolled and capered.

Unfortunately, when shoving off, the screw fouled a rope, passed from the steamer. The position was critical, but fortunately the rope broke, and with great care, by going very slowly, we reached the *Suvaroff*. Some one remarked, as I was dangling on the rope-ladder, choosing the moment to jump into the boat, " If only your wife could see you in that position ! " I was not in any actual danger.

The Governor lunched with the admiral to-day. He came on board in the *Alert*, a small steamer. He says that such winds are usual here.

If you only knew how sick I am of my surroundings! They say our cruise is a specially trying one; it has prejudiced me against the " beautiful " sea for ever. God grant that it end successfully! They will not entice me on board a sea-going ship again for a very long time. I have had enough of the sea—being torn away from home, living under unnatural conditions, everlasting surprises in the shape of breakages, damages, and repairs, dirt everywhere. You must not be surprised if I sometimes write ill-naturedly. My nerves are shaken a little, which is not surprising under the circumstances.

December 2nd.—To-day, for the first time, I saw

cormorants swimming at sea; I also saw a jelly-fish.

The officer commanding the German expedition and the commander of the native troops came to call on the admiral. The latter did not return the call himself, but sent the flag-captain. The *Orel* has lost an anchor and forty fathoms of cable. They are now grappling for them, as it was decided not to send down divers for fear of sharks.

December 3rd.—In the *Kamchatka* they obtained an English paper from a collier, in which it is related that the Japanese attacked the part of our fleet that is going *viâ* the Suez Canal, in or near the Red Sea. Our ships apparently received some damages. Perhaps this is a newspaper yarn. The *Roland* went to sea yesterday, to bury the body of a sailor who died in the *Korea*.

An order has been issued that we are to steam without any lights, in absolute darkness. Hitherto all lights were put out except distinctive lights—*i.e.* those absolutely necessary to show we are steaming. Now these are forbidden.

It is settled that we leave here to-morrow morning early.

What surprises are in store for us on the way to Madagascar? That there will be some is beyond doubt. I have been running round to-day like a squirrel in a cage. I went to the *Orel* and *Alexander*, and was, as usual, a long time in the *Borodino*.

The first lieutenant fell into a coal-shoot, hurt his leg, and is now laid up. It is very strange, whenever I go on board the *Borodino* my spirits go up. I have noticed this more than once, and it is always with pleasure that I go on board her.

Boats from every ship helped the *Orel* to search for her anchor and cable. They only found them to-day at three o'clock. They had, after all, to send divers down several times.

December 4th.—I have not slept well the last few days. I am inclined to sleep, but it is impossible to lie down. The rats have greatly increased on board. However, they afford a certain amount of fun. The dog Flagmansky (this name was given him because he came on board the same day as the staff) found a rat in one of the cabins, and chased it into a cupboard. Several men took an active part in the chase. All this time Flagmansky barked, whined, rushed into the corners, scratched at the cupboard, and bit it.

The hunt was not crowned with success, and he is still in the cabin guarding the rat. The cur has an extraordinary passion for rats. I put him into my cabin once (he begged to go there), and repented. He made such a disgraceful noise. For an hour and a half I could not drag him away. I had to call the orderly, who with great difficulty pulled him away from the cupboard.

CHAPTER IV

ON THE WAY TO MADAGASCAR

December 4th.—From Angra Pequena to Madagascar.

I only went to bed at 4 a.m., and rose at 8 a.m. We prepared to leave here at dawn, but at 1.30 a thick fog came on and continued till 9.30. As soon as it dispersed, the fleet weighed anchor. In the night a schooner came and lay near the fleet. The officer of the guard went on board. She is flying the English flag, and says she has come here for guano. Our next anchorage is at Madagascar, near the small island of St. Mary. This island lies near the north-eastern shores of Madagascar.

December 5th.—There was a short mass to-day.

A steamer was perceived far off going in our direction. Her funnel and two masts could only be seen from our masts. Perhaps she has come from St. Helena, and we may expect a surprise. At first she was noticed by the smoke from her funnel. She is now, no doubt, following us.

Something has happened to the *Aurora's* engines, but she has repaired it by now. To-day the *Suvaroff* steamed with one engine for a quarter of an hour.

Even the *Malay*, which has to be constantly nursed, is steaming successfully now. I expect several repairs were made when she was at Angra Pequena.

8 p.m.—The steamer which is on our course, though far away, overtook the fleet and went in the direction of Capetown.

December 6th.—To-day is December 6th. Where have I not spent this day? In Cronstadt, in Petersburg, in Tzarskoe Selo, in Tashkend, and in Gothland aboard the *Poltava*. Now I am spending it near the Cape of Good Hope. Who would believe that they would spend St. Nicholas Day near the southern coast of Africa? There was mass, prayers, and a salute. If foreigners heard it, no doubt it will appear in the papers that there was a fight, as firing had been heard.

We have not yet reached the Cape of Good Hope. We are just steaming past Capetown. Table Mountain is visible. The swell is tremendous. The ships are rolling. It is fearful to look at the *Nachimoff* and *Donskoi*, which are rolling especially heavily. The height of the waves sometimes reaches seventy feet. I was told this by the flag navigating officer. If we double the Cape in safety, then thanks be to God.

They have arranged a game for the crew. They hang up a bucket of water with a board attached to it, in which there is a hole. Those playing have, in passing under the bucket, to thrust a stick through the hole. This they seldom succeed in doing. Usually the stick hits the board, and the bucket is turned over, spilling the water on the player. The players are driven under the bucket on a field guncarriage.

We are steaming near the shore. It is hilly, dark, and treeless. Table Mountain is distinguished by its height and its summit, which is flat, as if the top of the mountain were cut off; this is apparently why it got its name. The Cape of Good Hope is a shapeless pile of cliffs. There is a lighthouse. We have now passed this cape and Capetown. To-night we shall be off Cape Agulhas. When we have passed it we shall have left the Atlantic and entered the Indian Ocean. We shall be able to say, one ocean passed; two more remain, the Indian and the Pacific. As the crow flies we are now at the greatest distance from Petersburg. Up to the present we have been going away from Japan, now we begin to approach. Near Capetown we met an enormous four-masted ship, flying the American flag. She was coming towards us. We are expecting to meet three suspicious schooners.

The weather is getting worse. In two hours we shall be on the same meridian as Petersburg; our time will be the same as it is there—that is, midnight. After this Petersburg time will be behind ours; hitherto it has been before. Evidently you cannot double the Cape without very bad weather. Perhaps it is all for the best, as it will be more difficult for the suspicious schooners to commit any hostile action.

Astern of the fleet and on the same course there is a steamer. At first she showed lights, now they are not visible. The moon is shining, but will soon set, and it will be quite dark. This will be the time to expect any unpleasant occurrences.

I hear the admiral does not want to take the small torpedo-boats with him, among them being the *Rezvy* (Sportive). Perhaps some of the officers of these boats will be transferred to other ships. It has been decided that the transports *Malay* and *Kniaz Gortchakoff* are to return to Russia from Madagascar. Their engines are bad, and have to be nursed continually.

All the fleet and auxiliary cruisers will assemble at Madagascar.

The same steamer is astern of us; she has her lights out. It is not merely out of curiosity she does this.

At first I used to be disturbed by reports of this kind, but am no longer. No doubt it is rather alarming, but nothing like it was before. How can this be explained? Nerves a little blunted, perhaps. It is summer here now. Nevertheless, at this time of the year ice sometimes drifts from the antarctic regions. They say a mountain of ice 100 feet above the water floated to the shore in summer-time.

December 7th.—Just as I sat down at table I was called away. It causes an unpleasant sensation when the engines race—that is, when the screws suddenly begin to turn very much quicker. This happens when there is no water over them, and is caused by the vessel pitching heavily; consequently, there is no resistance to their turning.

The steamer which has been following us all along is not to be seen. Perhaps towards night she will show herself somewhere. The wind has got up and raised a big sea. The sea is a following one. Great mountains of water pour on the upper deck. The ship is beginning to roll more heavily; we may expect a gale towards night if the wind strengthens. It is a good thing it is not a head sea—the ship steams more easily and does not roll so heavily. There is a lot of water on the deck in my cabin, as well as in other people's. I am now sitting with my legs huddled up. The water comes into the cabins through badly closed ports and badly riveted sides. The waves sometimes hit the side and make a noise like a shot from a gun. The weather is so bad that we need have no fear of being followed by the Japanese. They could no doubt attempt to fire a torpedo from the steamer, but it could hardly hit, and the steamer would certainly be fired on and sunk.

The battleships *Suvaroff, Alexander, Borodino,* and *Orel* have many defects which could be remedied in the construction of the *Slava* (Glory).

December 8th.—The weather was such yesterday that God grant we do not experience it a second time. Early in the morning it was tolerable, but later on the wind began to freshen. Standing on deck was difficult. The waves grew larger and larger—like immensely steep hills round the ship. They attained a height of forty feet.

From three to four o'clock the fury of the gale

reached its height. I am not sufficiently eloquent to describe it all. The ship tossed and groaned complainingly. Everything was tightly shut, but water came in everywhere. It poured in cascades on the upper deck, went into the turrets, stoke-holds, engine room, conning tower, and even on to the bridge. You could not walk on the poop, or you would be washed overboard. You could not breathe in the cabins; the atmosphere was like a bath (steam), if not worse. The wind roared, the ship rolled. The waves came up quite vertically—you looked and saw a wall of water. A boat which hung at the davits was smashed to bits, torn away, and carried off to sea.

Astern of the *Suvaroff* came the *Alexander*; at times, when the sea lifted the latter, her ram was visible. Sometimes her bows were at the bottom of a wave, and her stern at the top; and then all her deck, from bow to stern, could be seen from the *Suvaroff*. When I saw this I could not at first believe it. The best-behaved ship was the *Borodino*; she is a ship to be proud of.

At last the weather got to such a pitch that, had the engines or rudder of any ship given way, she would have been in a hopeless position. To think of help from other vessels would be useless. At this time each ship only thought of herself. The steamer *Roland* was flooded with waves minute after minute; she had to increase speed to escape them, and disappeared out of sight of the fleet.

She rejoined to-day. Thank God it was a following sea and a fair wind. What would it have been had it been a head or beam wind?

At 5 p.m. something went wrong with the engines of the *Malay*. She stopped and turned broadside to the wind. If you could but see what a sad sight she presented! It was impossible to help her, even if she had gone to the bottom before the eyes of the whole fleet. Nearly all the underwater part of her was visible. Wave after wave rolled over her. To help herself a little she set small and wretched sails. They were no good. The whole fleet, without lessening speed, went past the *Malay*, leaving her to cope by herself with the broken engine and the bad weather. Since then she has not been seen. How does she fare? It is not known whether she is afloat or sunk. We shall know nothing before we get to Madagascar. Perhaps all will yet be well.

The Indian Ocean has not given us a very affable reception. They were afraid that the wind would get up to-day, but although it is fresh it is tolerable. Storms such as we experienced yesterday last for a fortnight without a break. Last night, when the gale abated, rain squalls began to pass over us. This pleasure was not continuous; besides, we were wet enough without them. I went to bed late. I had wandered all over the ship. Went to sleep undressed. My feet had been wet through since the morning. While at lunch yesterday in the admiral's cabin a large wave rolled on to the upper deck; the door leading to the poop from the cabin had not been closed, and a cascade of water poured in. Every one raised their legs and kept them so until sailors had dried up the water. This wave was one of the first to fall on the ship.

What weather! You seldom see the like! I wrote to you that we had passed the meridian of Petersburg. I was mistaken. We only passed it to-day at 8 a.m.

December 9th.—The weather is gradually mending. The ship rolls lightly.

In the *Suvaroff* the cook and the messman were French. The messman left the ship at Vigo, and the former cook became messman. Every one grumbled at him. At last it was decided to get rid of him. One of the officers undertook to superintend the cooking. The messman will be put on shore at Madagascar.

Thanks to the favouring gale and fair wind we shall, it appears, reach Madagascar considerably earlier than was anticipated.

December 10th.—The weather is nearly quite calm, although the ship is still rolling slightly. At 8.30 the *Borodino* left the line. Something went wrong with her steering gear. She has not left the fleet, but is steaming alongside it. Now she has repaired the damage.

There are about 1,400 miles more to St. Mary, our next anchorage. Under favourable conditions we should arrive there in six or seven days. We shall get the mails and newspapers there. No news has been received about the *Malay*, though they call her up by signal in the evenings. If she has not suffered shipweck, she must be far from the fleet. Her speed is inconsiderable. We shall learn her fate at Madagascar.

December 11th.—During the night on board the *Suvaroff* the coal in the bunker caught fire. The fire was speedily extinguished with steam, which was injected into the bunker.

There is only a slight wind to-day, but the deadly swell continues. It is impossible to open the ports. Yesterday they brought my cap-covers from the wash. They are so torn now I can hardly wear them. You cannot imagine what a barbarous wash-house we have. They bring back the linen torn and stained. No matter how strong a material your tunic is made of, they tear it.

The *Orel* left the line, having damaged her steering engine; but she quickly set it right and resumed her place.

Just before the colours were lowered to-day a cloud appeared on the horizon, like smoke. They thought it was the *Malay* overtaking us. Our excitement appeared to have been needless. The *Kamchatka* complained of bad coal; she could not keep up sufficient steam, and began to drop astern. Her captain, by signal, asked permission to throw overboard some 150 tons of bad coal. The admiral, seeing in the fall of steam the work of some evil-disposed persons, refused, but gave permission to throw overboard the wrongdoer.

No sooner is the tale of the *Kamchatka* ended than the *Suvaroff* lies motionless, having damaged her steering engine. It was repaired somehow, and we proceeded.

December 12th.—A curious thing happened last night. They were communicating with the *Kamchatka* by signal. She hoisted a signal about her speed. The ship's signalmen interpreted the signal thus, "Do you see the torpedo-boats?" The officer of the watch sent down to wake all officers, and tell them that a torpedo-boat attack was imminent. Buglers and drummers were stationed to sound off quarters for action. There was general alarm.

A strong wind is beginning to blow. I hope it will not turn into a gale again, as it does not bring much joy. When you are ashore you pay no attention to the weather, whereas now you attentively follow its strength and direction. If nothing happens, there are four days' journey left to our anchorage in Madagascar. Up to the present we have come quicker than was intended. The storm on the eighth of the month helped us. At Madagascar the cruiser *Kuban* will probably join the fleet. She left Russia after we did. She outstripped us, and we have not yet seen her.

Probably at that island we shall be joined by the ships going by the Suez Canal. The weather is apparently about to get worse. The waves are again increasing. In the Atlantic it is calm; in the Indian Ocean it is always boisterous. They say that from Madagascar on it will be quieter. God grant it! It is impossible even for a minute to open one's port to let fresh air into the cabin. The artificial ventilation is very feeble.

ANOTHER STORM

December 13th.—Rain has fallen all to-day. The transport *Meteor* for some reason began to drop astern. (She is carrying fresh water. Although they distil water in the battleships and cruisers, she is nevertheless sometimes of assistance. She usually provides the transports with water.) Like all the other ships, she complains of the bad coal, with which it is difficult to keep up a sufficient quantity of steam for the boilers.

A storm has begun; the wind has suddenly freshened. Some say that this is a local squall, others that it is a cyclone. It is especially awkward for ships to get into a cyclone if they happen to be in its centre. Formerly sailing-ships that were caught in the centre of a cyclone seldom escaped. No doubt it is not so dangerous for steamships; yet, all the same, it may cause discomfort enough.

To-night is very dark. Black clouds stretch over the sky. The storm sometimes moves away, sometimes approaches us.

December 14th.—It was a cyclone yesterday; it only caught us with its circumference. Until one o'clock I was on deck. We are now passing along the eastern shore of Madagascar, and about thirty miles from it. The shore is clearly seen with the naked eye. It is high and mountainous. Just before twelve o'clock a steam-pipe burst in the stokehold of the *Suvaroff*. The steam whistled and began to pour into the stokehold. The men were nearly scalded. Some of them fled into the bunker, and shut the door behind them with the aid of a stoker, who remained in the stokehold and found a means of saving himself another way.

December 16th.—Off the island of St. Mary.

They have brought news from the shore. Ay! such news that the remembrance of it is nauseating. All the ships at Port Arthur are destroyed. The *Gromoboy* (Thunderer) has struck on the rocks. Kuropatkin sits tight at Mukden and organises parades. A third deep-sea fleet is leaving, or preparing to leave, Libau. Can this be true? What is all this? Are they joking, or have they quite lost their heads? You cannot imagine how mortifying it is. Everywhere are failures, corruption, stupidity, and mistakes. No doubt you, living in Petersburg, have heard all gradually. It all falls on us as a sudden blow. Involuntarily you are overwhelmed with horror. There is not one bright spot; all around is hopeless darkness.

Yes, our affairs are bad, very bad!

The steamer *Roland* is going to the town of Tamatave, which is about a hundred versts from our anchorage. The hospital-ship *Orel* arrived from Capetown and brought newspapers. The officers of the *Orel* say that in the streets of Capetown you constantly hear Russian spoken; that is, by Jews from Russia. There are some thirteen and a half thousands of them. Many of them have fled from Russia in order to escape their military obligations. The Jews so besieged the *Orel*, wishing to look over her, that at last the police had to drive them away from the ship.

December 17th.—The *Roland*, when coming out of Tamatave, signalled that the *Malay* was coming in. A schooner flying the Swiss flag has arrived here—schooner of a country where there is no sea!

The *Malay* has arrived. It does not do to believe all the news from the fleet. For instance, to-day a telegram was sent *viâ* Tamatave, saying we had coaled near Durban. Nothing of the kind occurred. It was telegraphed to alarm the English and compel them to institute an inquiry. In one word, to make them show that they had not broken their neutrality.

The *Orel* brought the captain of the *Suvaroff* the *Novoe Vremya* (New Times) and *Birgevya Viedomosti* (Bourse News) from Capetown. How eagerly we read them!

Our fleet lies in the strait between the islands of Madagascar and St. Mary. To-day we were informed from St. Mary that two ships were lying on the other side. Was it from these ships we received signals? They suppose them to be Japanese cruisers, and fear for the *Roland*. She has not returned. If there are Japanese cruisers here they might easily catch her and send her to the bottom.

It is very probable that the ships coming *viâ* Suez are lying in the Mozambique Channel, off Madagascar (near the western shore). As yet we have no news of them.

December 18th.—To-day the admiral and several officers of his staff went to the island of St. Mary. I did not want to go, so did not take advantage of the opportunity. The steamer *Esperanza*, which is bringing provisions for the fleet, has not yet arrived. She had to call at Capetown, and then follow us here. Perhaps we shall remain off the island here for a prolonged time. Evidently the term of our stay depends on the answer to the telegram sent to Petersburg.

To-morrow a steamer arrives (French), and leaves on the 21st, taking the mails.

The *Roland* has not yet returned. Where the rest of the ships are is not known.

The question of the return to Russia of the *Malay* is definitely settled. She is to go to the Black Sea. Her stores will be taken in the other transports. She goes from here *viâ* the Suez Canal, taking the sick and feeble from the fleet. That will be one burden the less.

December 19th.—I have been to St. Mary to-day. The trip began by our scarcely reaching the shore. It was rough, and a head sea began to pour over the cutter. I was wet through, and cursed myself for coming.

The scenery here is very little different from Gaboon and Dakar. There is the same rich tropical growth. The types of inhabitants are different. The people here dress more than those at Gaboon, and appear well built. The population does not enjoy the confidence of the French, and the soldiers are taken from another place. Not long ago the natives killed two European officers in Madagascar. When our fleet arrived, they thought we had come to punish them for the murders, and several settlements ran away. St. Mary is a Sagalien for Madagascar. There are two prisons— one for political offenders, the other for capital offenders. What strikes one generally about the negroes is their gait. They walk holding themselves upright.

I wandered about on shore, was in the village, and looked into the church (Roman Catholic). It is the new year to-day, according to the New Style. The population are dressed in their holiday clothes. I bought six very pretty shells in the village for a franc. Strolling along the beach I collected fifty shells—one large one of six to eight inches diameter. My walk along the beach was poisoned by anticipation of having to row back to the ship, which, with the others, lies very far from the shore.

I went on board the ship, and there was a surprise for me—to go to the *Esperanza*, which had only just arrived. The weather had already grown much rougher. Two Frenchmen have come aboard the *Suvaroff*, and they cannot get ashore; they will have to spend the night here. The sailors from their boat are negroes, and have been sent to sleep with the crew, whose chance guests afford them amusement.

In the morning the *Roland* arrived, and brought the news that they had seen a suspicious schooner and a destroyer (Japanese). They saw Admiral Folkersham's fleet (which came by Suez) had gone to Nosi Be. No answer had been received at Tamatave from Petersburg. A French steamer will bring us the answer to-morrow. At Tamatave the French gave our officers a friendly reception. On the occasion of the arrival of the Russian fleet they even printed the menus with the double-headed eagle and our flags.

December 20th.—I was called early this morning. I have to go to the *Esperanza* again. I am wet through, and have to change my clothes and boots. It is a good thing that those I wore yesterday have dried. The Frenchmen have gone and taken with them the letters and telegrams to give to the steamer. I missed the dispatch of letters owing to the trip to the *Esperanza*.

Our fleet will soon shift its anchorage. We shall hardly go to Nosi Be. It is awkward to lie there, and the bay is shallow for battleships and also for transports. The refrigerator in the *Esperanza*, which cools the air in the holds where the meat is stowed, is damaged. This is unfortunate; the meat will go bad, and we shall have to feed on salt meat.

At four o'clock the steamer *Pernosbucco* arrived here; she brought no news from Petersburg. At seven she left for Diego Suarez. To-morrow we get up anchor and go north to some bay.

A stoker died on board the *Oslyabya*; he was buried at five o'clock to-day. The *Oslyabya* left the line, half-masted her colours, fired her guns (a salute), and committed the body to the sea. During this ceremony the officers and crews of all the ships stood at "attention," and where there were bands they played "Kol Slaven." [1]

To-day the wireless station received some signals, evidently sent from a great distance. None of the ships could decipher them—it was not known, even, in what language they were written. To-morrow I shall learn whether it was not one of our newly arrived ships that signalled.

December 21st.—In the bay of Tang-tang.

This morning we weighed and shifted from St. Mary nearer to Madagascar, in the bay of Tang-tang. It is better protected than where we were lying.

The guns are ready at any minute to commence firing. In all corners of the ship are men talking in undertones. They anxiously scan the horizon. The outlines of the nearest ships stand out in black silhouettes. At the sides the torpedo-nets are rocked by the waves. The searchlights are ready to instantly illuminate all around. The tension is felt, though there is absolute stillness. Every one is chilled by fearful anticipation.

December 22nd.—To-day the cruiser *Kuban* is

[1] A funeral march.

expected to arrive, and to-morrow the squadron that came *viâ* Suez.

In the English newspapers there is an announcement that Russia has ordered thirty ships of various kinds in Germany and Italy.

Those undeciphered signals which our wireless stations received have been made out by some one in the *Nachimoff*. The signal was Japanese. It stated that "the Russian fleet is lying without lights off the island of St. Mary." To-day a French officer commanding some local troops arrived, and spent the night on board the *Suvaroff*. The torpedo-nets were again got out; the crews were at their guns; steam and mining cutters lay near their ships, one-third of the officers were on deck by order, and a large number out of curiosity.

The night was rather dark—half the sky was covered with clouds. Occasionally sparks of light glimmer here and there. Some one is signalling. A light flashes on shore; it is answered from the sea. The *Aurora* reports that she saw six lights astern of her. I myself saw four out at sea and one on shore. What will to-night bring us? An attack must be expected. Everything is so unusual. All lights are hidden. At dawn a cruiser is leaving with secret orders, apparently for the colliers.

December 23rd.—The *Malay*, which remained at our former anchorage, has not yet reached the fleet. The cruisers have gone. The *Roland* has not yet returned. The *Kuban* is not here, nor the squadron from Suez. To-night there was a long story from the *Esperanza*, which is cruising under the French flag and has a French crew. The crew, not liking to lie at anchor without lights during the night, threatened the captain. These brave Frenchmen feared an attack. The *Esperanza* has now been sent away somewhere. A collier arrived bringing some information, thanks to which we shall leave here to-morrow—whither I do not yet know.

Evening.—The *Kuban*, it appears, is lying at Diego Suarez, and the ships from Suez at Nosi Be, where we are also going to-morrow.

December 24th.—Port Arthur has surrendered. What more can be said?

On the way to Nosi Be from Tang-tang.

The sad news of the surrender of Port Arthur was brought by the *Roland*. She arrived to-day.

On the 24th the cruiser *Svietlana* and the torpedo-boats *Biedovy* and *Bodry* joined the fleet. The latter damaged her engines, and was at once taken in tow by the *Roland*. The same day we met two colliers. They were ordered to go to Nosi Be. On the 25th the *Bodry* reported that she had very little coal. The fleet stopped, and the *Bodry* took coal from the *Anadir*, going alongside her.

It is a good thing it was calm, and this could be done without risk of damage. Yesterday there was mass and prayers. It is really Christmas. After mass the admiral made a short but impressive speech to the crew. All the ships saluted according to regulation. They fired thirty-one guns.

In the evening the *Borodino* reported by semaphore that shortly before sunset four large warships were visible from her masts, steaming in line ahead. Afterwards three of the ships turned and disappeared. Lights were burning on the remaining ship. After a short time, they made out that this ship, having put out her lights, altered course and also disappeared. There is evidence that there are Japanese warships off Madagascar. The night passed in alarms. Some lights were visible away from our course. Attacks were feared. Instructions were given to the battleships and transports what to do during an attack.

The cruiser *Svietlana* was sent to the squadron lying in Nosi Be.

I could not sleep from the closeness in my cabin. Until 6 a.m. I slept in my clothes on a sofa in the wardroom. At 6 I went back to my cabin and opened the port. The sea wetted the table and fell on to the bed, but that afforded nothing but pleasure. It does not even wake you.

This morning we got into communication by wireless with the *Svietlana*, which is ahead of the fleet, while she was in communication with the squadron at Nosi Be. It appears that our cruisers *Aurora*, *Donskoi*, and *Nachimoff* are lying there. Yesterday it was supposed that the ships seen in line ahead were these cruisers and the *Kuban*, which joined them from Diego Suarez. Now this supposition falls to the ground.

We are going by a spot seldom explored and not sounded. Occasionally shallow places are shown on the chart, and the fairway along which we are steaming is very narrow; the depth is unknown—it has not been measured. We may go aground.

To-day I finished writing those reports about the battleships *Borodino, Orel, Imperator Alexander III.*, and *Kniaz Suvaroff*, which I began long ago. I must touch them up a little and send them to Petersburg. Many will be dissatisfied with them, and probably I shall make enemies for myself. No matter. Having once decided on it, I must carry it out—the more so as it appears to me the remarks will be very useful.

At seven o'clock the torpedo-boat *Buiny* (Boisterous) approached, coming from Nosi Be. All is well there. The torpedo-boat offered to escort the hospital-ship *Orel* to the anchorage. At present our fleet is thirty miles from the anchorage. Owing to the dangerous entrance, we shall remain at sea all night, and go in to-morrow morning. Tossing on the sea all night with the transports is not without danger.

December 27th.—The fleet is steaming slowly, turning constantly in order not to be too far off Nosi Be. At 2 p.m. the *Roland* hoisted a signal, "The crew have mutinied." The torpedo-boat *Biedovy* was ordered to reduce the mutineers to submission, and if necessary to shoot them. The torpedo-boat, with such full powers, soon re-established order. It appeared that the stokers did not wish to take the place of two sick comrades, and hence the whole story.

I hardly slept all night. Went to bed at four and got up at seven. We are approaching our anchorage. What news awaits us? After the destruction of the fleet and the fall of Port Arthur, affairs are radically changed. There is now no need for haste.

There are three courses open to our fleet—either to continue the voyage to the East, to remain for an indefinite time in some place in the expectation that its presence will be necessary on the coast of Japan, or to return to Russia. If we are obliged to remain somewhere and wait, will the admiral remain in the fleet? And if he goes, what fate may his staff expect?

I had just sat down and busied myself when I heard the sound of my beloved Little Russian march. I looked out of my port and saw we had arrived at Nosi Be. I ran on deck and saw a wonderful picture. The bay, the calm sea, hills all round—two of the latter especially, covered with a thick wood, stand at the entrance opposite each other. The sun is scorching. In the bay are the remains of the naval might of our unfortunate fatherland. The sounds of the march re-echo. We have rejoined all the ships that we parted from at Tangier more than two months ago. Here are all that are left to Russia. Can it be that they will be ingloriously and ignominiously destroyed? The fleet is still strong enough, but is it efficient? There were more ships, and they are battered to pieces or lie at the bottom of the sea. Can it be that our fleet will complete the great tragedy of the ruin of an immense navy?

The meeting of our admiral and Admiral Folkersham was very hearty. They embraced. You cannot recognise the men in the boats of Admiral Folkersham's division. They are all in sun helmets, whereas our men have put neck-covers on their caps. Admirals Folkersham and Enquist were invited to lunch. They learnt the news. All are sad.

There is neither telegraph nor post here. Torpedo-boats go to Mayung (Mojanga) in order to send the mails and telegrams. It is about 200 versts from here. There are few Europeans. We hear occasional newspaper reports which we do not know how to believe. One is perfectly terrible. Port Arthur surrendered with a garrison of more than 40,000 men, among whom were 1,000 officers. It is simply incredible! The triumph of the Japanese is complete; they will raise our ships that were sunk in Port Arthur harbour, and leaving them their former names, will fight in them against us.

Admiral Folkersham says there are no mails or letters from Russia. He telegraphed twice to our staff requesting them to send on letters. They did not even reply. What is it to them, sitting snugly in Petersburg, that more than 850 officers alone have no news from home for two months ? It is all the same to them ! They are all right, and as regards others it is not their business.

They do not count on taking the transports *Gortchakoff* and *Malay* any further, but will send them to Russia from here. It is said that, according to the first order, the fleet is to leave Madagascar on January 1st. The captain of the torpedo-boat *Buiny* has come. There are several breakages and defects in this boat. I shall have to go to-morrow morning and make arrangements for their repair.

We have a tremendous voyage before us—across the Indian Ocean, calling nowhere. Under favourable conditions we shall get to the East Indian Archipelago in twenty days, and then Japan is quite close. What will it be ? Can the fate of the Port Arthur fleet await us ? It is said that Nosi Be is extraordinarily like the harbour of Nagasaki. It is not possible to remain in one's cabin. The deck is so hot that you can feel the heat through the soles of your boots.

The cyclone that overtook us on the way to Madagascar apparently caused much damage in this island. Thank God that we came happily out of it. The cruise in the ships that came *viâ* Suez was much easier than ours. They called at well-constructed ports. The voyage was shorter. Officers and men were frequently allowed ashore. Our fleet accomplishéd a tremendous voyage, calling at a few deserted bays. The crew were not allowed on shore, and the officers seldom had permission to land. It is said permission to land will be given to-morrow. It does not attract me; the shore is wild and deserted.

To-night I can sleep with my port open. I shall be able to breathe. I must go to bed early. It is already late, and to-morrow I must get up early, and dash round the ships. At present there are few damages. Perhaps they have not been able to report them. I shall see to-morrow.

CHAPTER V

AT MADAGASCAR

DECEMBER 28*th*.—Since early this morning I have been visiting ships. Here is a description of life in a torpedo-boat,—crowded, dirty, hot, and always rolling; the decks littered with various things, the crew sleeping in every corner. Dogs are crowded together, and in several boats there are monkeys. There is nowhere to walk. The crew—good, resolute, bold, and crafty—are crowded with the officers, but do not inconvenience them.

I called on the *Borodino* and went into the wardroom and captain's cabin. During the last voyage they got up theatricals for the amusement of the crew. They were very successful. The clowns especially excelled; they say they were as good as professionals.

The sun here scorches one severely. I descended from the *Kamchatka,* sat on the wooden thwart of the cutter, and jumped up quickly—I had burnt myself.

December 29th.—To-day from 12.30 I was on shore with the captain, buying wood. We were at a German factory, and I asked the Germans to send a letter when opportunity offered. I think they may be depended on.

Letter No. 74 was sent by collier to Port Said, where the mail will be handed over to the Consul, and he will dispatch them to the staff, who will forward them to the addresses—a lengthy procedure. A steamer has arrived with provisions (the *Esperanza*).

On shore I saw a negro suffering from the so-called elephantiasis. His legs were swollen, and were as thick as wooden posts. The disease only attacks negroes and Malays.

I wonder what telegrams the admiral has received? A French torpedo-boat brought some service telegrams, as well as private ones, from Mayung (Mojanga). The former are, of course, in cipher. They are deciphering them now.

My servant has just come to ask me to change his Russian money for French money. I gave him five francs. There is very little foreign money in the fleet, and great trouble in changing Russian. No decision as to the fate of our fleet has been received from Petersburg. They are silent—perhaps they are consulting.

Three officers have been discharged from the fleet: an ensign who went mad, a lieutenant through illness, and the paymaster of the *Aurora*. A court of inquiry has been appointed to survey the transports *Malay* and *Kniaz Gortchakoff*, which are being sent to Russia. I am one of the members. I wanted to go ashore to-morrow, but shall not be able, owing to this inquiry. It is very trying, having to remain waiting the decision of the fate of the fleet from Petersburg.

December 30th.—I was unable to finish my letter yesterday, as I was sent to the *Borodino*. I went there at twelve, midnight. An unfortunate accident occured. Two sailors went into the wing passage and were suffocated, although the manhole was open. The closeness in these passages is frightful —there is little air, and poisonous gases accumulate. The sailors, in my opinion, became weak, could not lift themselves up the ladder, fell, struck their heads on something, and were suffocated. They wanted to make a post-mortem on the deceased, but did not do so.

I passed the night in the *Borodino*, in the

admiral's dining-cabin on a sofa. At six I got up, having slept for two or three hours. They provided me with a mat and a pillow. It was fearfully hot and stuffy, although the doors and ports were open. The heat is unbearable. You are always wet with perspiration. Yesterday I saw a case of sickness from the heat. A writer was taken ill at night, though it was cooler then than in the day.

A sailor in the *Suvaroff* was also nearly suffocated in the wing passage. Sunstrokes are frequent. I called this morning at the *Suvaroff*, and was immediately sent on board the *Malay* for the inquiry. While there I was twice sent for by the admiral. He wrote a severe order about the death of the two sailors in the *Borodino*. He ordered me to add to this order some technical details. Taking advantage of this, I toned the order down as much as I could in sending it to be printed.

At four o'clock the dead sailors from the *Borodino* were buried. The admiral was present at the requiem service. Their bodies were taken in a boat to the torpedo-boat *Bravy*. She took them further out to sea and committed them to the deep. It was a sad ceremony. When the cutter shoved off from the *Borodino* with the bodies, they fired guns; the band played the funeral march, "Kol Slaven." The officers and crews of all the ships stood at "attention."

Phew! how stuffy! I can scarcely write. In the *Borodino* I saw that the officers, to escape the heat, slept on deck among the coal, like the crew, undressed and dirty. The beds of the officers are only distinguished from those of the crew by being mats. When I first saw this sleeping company I could hardly believe my eyes.

What an unfortunate day it has been for the *Ural*! In the morning a sailor had a sunstroke, and in the evening two officers, an ensign and a lieutenant, were struck by the traveller of the Temperley,[1] which had carried away. The ensign was killed on the spot—his chest was crushed and his spine broken. There is still hope of saving the lieutenant. He received a blow on the head, and fell down unconscious; it may be he will pull through. It is a strange thing about this lieutenant. He is a Black Sea officer, and has only just come to the *Ural*. He was sent from the Black Sea at half an hour's notice to this cruiser. You see many officers in the fleet, but his Black Sea cap (all white

[1] An apparatus for hoisting coal in bags out of colliers into the ships.

with a peak) attracted the eye. He was on board the *Suvaroff* an hour before the accident. They induced him to remain; he was late for his watch; but all the same, to his misfortune, he went to his ship. When he came on board us he met some comrades, told them a lot about the Black Sea fleet, abused it and its personnel. I was sitting near and was an involuntary listener. His stories interested me. Abusing the personnel, he related how three of his comrades with whom he lived made an end of their lives. "See," he said, "I lived with four comrades, and three of them have put an end to their lives, and something of the same kind will happen to me." He said this about an hour before the accident. For a few minutes before his departure I talked to him, and he told me how he had come to the *Ural*.

There is a great talk in the wardroom now about the *Suvaroff* being forbidden communication with the shore, because a sailor was absent and they made no attempt to find him. In every ship you must look out for animals—parrots, monkeys, oxen, chicken, geese, chameleons, frogs, pigs, and dogs; in a word, every sort is collected together. In one of the ships they brought a snake in the hay for the cattle. It bit an engineer in the breast, which swelled tremendously. They feared he would die. Now he is all right; the swelling has subsided.

It is late; I must go and try to sleep. Haven't slept much for the last two nights.

December 31*st.*—There has been a great deal of talk about the sending of money to Russia for the crew. It cannot be managed. New Year's Eve is on us, but the days are so much alike that no one ever thought about it up to the present time. The sailor who had sunstroke died, and after death the temperature of his body was 43° R.

I had scarcely finished my letter when I had to go in the cutter to the *Ural*. The *Ural* is one of the steamers bought from the Germans. She is very well finished. In the saloons are paintings, gilt and carved decorations. She is very big.

I went below, and the requiem service began. I shall not forget it soon. Here were joined luxury and poverty, elegance and squalor. The church is the former first-class saloon, now the wardroom, turned into a shrine. Eight large fans made a peculiar noise in quick time. A crowd of officers were there, dressed in white. The choir sang almost a gay chant—badly, but in tune; the priest helped them. During the pauses the dull noise of the fans was clearly heard. There were sentries on both sides of the coffin, which rested on a rude table, not covered with anything. It was more like a box than coffin, and had been made roughly out of pine boards, badly painted. The wood showed through the paint in streaks. During the service they sewed the coffin up in white calico. They could not find a whole piece, so added scraps. The wreaths were composed of fresh flowers.

A sad spectacle. Apparently the ensign was not killed by the traveller, but by the Temperley itself. After the service the coffin was lowered into the boat by the very Temperley that wrought the accident. A steam cutter towed the boat to the shore, and was followed by a long line of boats, filled with the funeral party. When the coffin was being lowered, they fired a gun, and all ships put their ensigns at half-mast. The crews stood at "attention," and the band played the funeral march.

Two bands awaited the procession on shore; they had accompanied the other dead man. This was the sailor (from the same *Ural*) who died from sunstroke. At the cemetery the funeral service was read, the coffins lowered into the graves, and the escort fired three volleys. Simple crosses were erected, and then all dispersed. They left behind two Russians to lie in their graves, far from their fatherland, among strangers, under simple white crosses with a crooked and uneven superscription roughly carved on them. Little did they think that fate would send them death far from Russia in a strange country, in the midst of luxurious though foreign nature! Little did they think that they would lie side by side—that both would be buried in the same hour. Indeed, one cannot escape fate.

Another sailor has gone mad in the *Orel.*

But enough of this. . . .

January 1st.—I left the wardroom at four o'clock. Many remained and occupied themselves in drinking. I returned on board the *Suvaroff* yesterday, in the *Borodino's* boat.

The population of Nosi Be is a mixed one. You may meet negroes, Malays, Jews, Indians, and a few Europeans. Horses are scarce, and you travel in litters borne on the shoulders of men.

There are numerous breeds of monkeys, parrots, lizards, crocodiles, etc.

Cattle are plentiful; the oxen have humps, and immense horns. Yesterday a scene occurred with the oxen! When the funeral procession came up to the cart, to which oxen were harnessed, the band was playing. The oxen were frightened and ran wild. One tore himself away from the yoke and charged the firing-party following the coffin, with lowered horns. A catastrophe was narrowly averted. They soon succeeded in driving him away. The other struggled for a long while in the yoke, and at last got free.

Chosen officers are going from each ship to all the others with congratulations. It is evident that they will return to their ships late, and not quite themselves. They are treated generously, and offence is taken if they drink too little.

A torpedo-boat has arrived from Mojanga with telegrams; some are cipher telegrams from Petersburg—they have not yet read them. There is news that the *Oleg* passed through the Suez Canal on the 31st. If that is so, she may arrive here on the 22nd inst.

Am just going round the ships.

January 2nd.—The *Kuban* has arrived. To-morrow I may go on board her. I have journeyed somewhat to-day. After lunch I went to the *Aurora, Nachimoff, Jemchug, Sissoi,* and *Voronej.* The latter belongs to the volunteer fleet. On board her I procured a thousand cigarettes for ten roubles. I was much pleased with this. In going on board the *Aurora* I lost the top of my helmet. It acted as a ventilator, and cannot be replaced. I must go about without it.

Several of us, I among the number, have prickly heat. It is not very disquieting, but at the same time does not afford any pleasure. In the *Jemchug*, where I have not been since Libau, they did not recognise me. I am so changed in face, owing to my beard.

We remain here, and know nothing of when and where we are going. Probably we shall wait for the *Oleg*, *Isumrud*, and torpedo-boats. Persistent rumours are floating about that the fleet will return. Letters have been received from Sevastopol with very bad news. It is said that the sailors there have mutinied and created much trouble. They say there are serious disorders in Petersburg.

To-day I should have gone to some ships, but could not, as all the boats were away for the exercise of landing parties. Finished my work, "Notes on Ships of the *Borodino* Type." Handed them into the office to be typewritten. If it is true that we leave on the 6th or 7th, I shall hardly be able to send them to Petersburg. Can it be that we shall not wait for the *Oleg* and other ships coming with her? That would be idiotic! To stay quietly and strengthen the fleet does not interfere with the cruisers and torpedo-boats.

January 3rd.—What a day it has been! I scarcely got through lunch when, at two o'clock, I went to the *Donskoi*, from there to the *Borodino*, and then to the *Ural*. Have only just returned to the *Suvaroff*, having had nothing to eat anywhere, and now only bread-and-butter. It is a good thing I fortified myself with chocolate. The *Ural* is the former steamer *Queen Maria Theresa*. She ran between Hamburg and America.

There are a lot of sick in the fleet; two belong to the staff, the flag engineer and the flag intendant. The senior auditor is sick, but is doing his duty. It is the fault of this climate.

January 4th.—I have been to the *Kuban*, which was formerly a German passenger steamer and ran across the Atlantic Ocean. She has all the conveniences of life, is roomy and luxurious, but as a warship the *Kuban*, like the other purchased ships, is useless. She has few guns; their calibre is small, and there is no armoured protection. All is wood.

More animals have made their appearance in the ship. They have brought a hare, a porcupine, and a dog off from the shore. Wherever you look now you see birds, beasts, or vermin. On deck oxen are standing ready to be slaughtered for meat, to say nothing of fowls, geese, and ducks. In the cabins are monkeys, parrots, and chameleons.

Having scratched you a letter, I went to put it with some postcards into the box. At the post-office were crowds of people, hurrying to post letters to catch the outgoing steamer. I scarcely waited to buy stamps for the postcards. As stamps would stick together while being kept, those having greater values are not covered with gum. This is very inconvenient, as you have not always gum at hand. I had to buy some gum-arabic in a shop. Indians are the principal shopkeepers here. Boys in the street call out simple words of Russian, and frequently repeat them. Profiting by the arrival of the fleet, everything is dreadfully dear. They have never before done such a roaring trade. One of the places here has a high-sounding name—" Parisian Café." The landlord of this café says that after the departure of the fleet he will close it and go to Paris. He will never earn more than now.

From the post-office I went to this café. They persuaded me to play vint (Russian whist). Close by were a lot of officers playing macao. They play very high (during our stay at Nosi Be one officer succeeded in losing more than £400—*i.e.*

4000 roubles). I did not sit down to play macao; but just trifled with it, lost sixty francs, and then went to the quay. It was time—just six o'clock—and the boat was due to shove off. By seven I was on board, having been on shore less than four hours. On going into my cabin I learnt some news. We leave on the 7th. The post was sent by Günsburg. Whether we leave Madagascar on the 7th, or are only going to change our anchorage, I do not know. Either is possible.

January 5th.—I went on shore to-day. There was a large crowd around the post-office, all Russians. Some were posting letters, others buying stamps. I thought I would go into a café to get a drink. I asked for a bottle of soda-water with ice, and squeezed a grenadine into it. For this they charged four francs.

I left the café and went to the cemetery, where the Russians and other Europeans were buried, and sat there awhile. It is a poor place, all overgrown. The memorial crosses are the only white spots. Everything is sunk, hidden by the tropical growth. It is almost a forest. Many birds flutter about in the trees—some remarkably pretty, with rich plumage of all colours. I saw a colibri there (the smallest bird in the world). I used to think they were considerably smaller than they actually are.

From the cemetery I returned to the post-office. My companion lost all hope of posting his letter, so many were waiting their turn. I persuaded him to remain, and we managed to do our business there. We went to the quay, but the boat was not there. We had to wait, so, being tormented by thirst, we went to the café. I drank a bottle of lemonade, and my companion a bottle of beer, and it cost four francs. A bottle of champagne costs forty francs—*i.e.* about fifteen roubles.

In every corner of the café officers from the fleet are sitting at tables and playing cards, vint and macao. At three tables macao was being played for heavy stakes. French officers from the torpedo gunboat looked on in astonishment. I did not play.

Several men obtained riding-horses and mules—tired, broken, and lean beasts. A large number of officers from the *Borodino* walked through a virgin forest, forcing their way through the lianas. They made themselves very dirty. Two officers from the *Suvaroff* went out shooting, but bagged nothing. At seven o'clock I returned on board, fairly tired, having walked nearly all day.

January 6th.—Although I was tired, I went to bed last night at twelve. It rained all night. This cooled our hot sides, which do not generally grow cool during the night.

Now there are constant rain squalls. There was mass, prayers, and the blessing of the water to-day. The priest made a procession to sprinkle the ensign and the jack.[1] There was chicken pie for lunch, but a very inferior one. The French torpedo-boat again brought official telegrams. They have not yet been deciphered: perhaps they contain something interesting.

January 7th.—Yesterday a steam cutter from the *Donskoi* went aground. They got her off to-day.

A native came and complained that a boat from the fleet had sunk his catamaran (native boat), in which was a case of champagne, a case of rum, and a box of lemons. He was probably indemnified.

I had just sat down to write when I was required to go on board the *Jemchug*. Just returned.

The ladies' committee of the "Society to help the Wounded" sent the admiral the ikon of St. George "the Victorious," and fifty small crosses for the officers and crew. I received a cross and hung it

[1] A small flag flown in the bow of the ship when at anchor.

to a chain with my own. It is very pretty, and made of mother-of-pearl.

The rainy season, which should have begun a fortnight ago, was late. It has now begun—another pleasure for us.

Many of the wardroom tumblers are broken. They cannot be bought here. Jam-pots are used instead.

It is difficult to imagine how the local traders live. They have raised all prices considerably, and continue to raise them.

The provision-ship *Esperanza* will no longer accompany the fleet. I wanted to go ashore at 6 a.m. to-morrow with some one, to explore the interior of the island; but it is impossible. An inquiry is to be held in the *Malay* to survey the coal left in her. I have to take a part in this inquiry.

Again there are rumours that the fleet will leave here on the 11th. I think this is only supposition. The French mail-steamer leaves for Europe on the 9th. Perhaps this letter will be the last that will go in her. There will then be a break in my letters. Steamers do not often call here—only once or twice a month.

Some chameleons were brought on board, and

have now spread all over the ship. They are harmless; but to me, at all events, they are repulsive. Some fellows take them in their hands and allow them to crawl over their heads and faces.

January 8th.—Since 4 a.m. there has been such a downpour, difficult to imagine if you have not seen it. Many men, desiring to wash in fresh water, took advantage of the rain to go on deck with a piece of soap and wash themselves.

At this blessed moment I have to go to the inquiry in the *Malay*.

While I was standing at a closed hatchway on deck, waiting for the captain of the *Malay*, a man was wandering about in white uniform, bare-footed and capless. I paid no attention to him. Suddenly he approached me and stretched out his hand. I hesitated, thinking he was a drunken sailor playing a joke. "I knew you very well long ago. I am Titoff," he said. Then I guessed that this was the mad ensign from the battleship *Orel*. I shook hands with him, and said that I had not recognised him because he had grown a beard, although in deed it was only of two or three days' growth. He began to laugh, asked me if I feared Death, and had I seen him; and, pointing all round, he said, "This is all Russia," etc. They were not very pleasant minutes that I spent in his company. It was sad to see him. He walks about the dirty deck half undressed. He does what he likes. He may fall overboard, or fall down a hatchway, or slip from a ladder—no one looks after him. A melancholy spectacle!

I returned to the *Suvaroff* from the *Malay* at twelve o'clock. I was hot and tired. Now the sun's rays are nearly vertical. I wetted my head with salt water and put a wet handkerchief in my cap. The leather of my boots burnt my feet. I found a letter from the captain of the *Jemchug* awaiting me. I must go there and to the *Donskoi*. I am tired of going to the latter; I have to go there nearly every day. I lunched in my cabin. The orderly who waited on me said, "I have brought you a beetle."[1] I did not understand at first what he meant. Apparently it was a block of wood to put under the feet when sitting at the writing-table.

6 p.m.—Have been to the *Gortchakoff*, *Borodino*, *Donskoi*, and *Jemchug*. In the latter they are also using jam-pots as tumblers. It is a wearisome cruise. Officers and men have so many inconveniences and discomforts to bear.

A fine company are collected in the *Malay* to

[1] An implement used by washerwomen.

go back to Russia—the sick, prisoners, men dismissed from the service, lunatics, and drunkards. The captain has already reported that they do not obey him—abuse and threaten to kill him. Their conduct is defiant, and they will not submit to any orders. If they do not send a trusty guard he will always have to carry a loaded revolver, and shoot the first one who disobeys. In this steamer a strong and firm captain is required in order to reach a Russian port in safety with such a crew.

A court for trying offences during the voyage was appointed to the fleet. To-day this court assembled to try a sailor of the *Suvaroff*. He had abused the chief boatswain, threatened, and disobeyed the orders of the first lieutenant. He was sentenced to three and a half years in a disciplinary battalion. Probably he will be sent to Russia in the *Malay*.

January 9th.—The foreboding about the *Malay* is beginning to be justified. Last night an armed crew had to be sent to arrest the mutineers. They arrested four of the *Malay's* hired crew. These have been divided among the battleships, in order that they may be put in cells. The most insolent is on board the *Suvaroff*. The appearance of the armed crew in the *Malay* produced a great sensation. The rest of her crew instantly quieted down. They evidently had not expected the matter to end in this sad way.

After those arrested have done some days in cells, it has been decided to put them on shore and abandon them to the dictates of fate. To be in cells on board the *Borodino* is tolerable, but in the *Suvaroff*, "God forbid!" The temperature there is fearful, and there is no ventilation. I do not think that a man could remain there long. Among the four prisoners one only is the ringleader. It is he who is in the *Suvaroff*. One of them actually cried. To be cast upon a nearly desert shore! What will they do? There is no employment for them, and they lack the means of getting away. Could they join the foreign legion? It is not here, now that this place is unimportant.

I have not told you what the foreign legion is. The French Government only enlists foreigners in it. It is stationed in wild places in the colonies where the population is unsettled. Desperate men, criminals, escaped convicts, and adventurers serve in it. On entering it they do not ask for passports, nor do they inquire into antecedents. In it are to be met representatives of every nation and of every grade of society. Its ranks consist of common soldiers, aristocrats, officers, and hawkers. Discipline in the legion is very strict in order to keep this rabble in submission. There are said to be many Russians in it. The legion was stationed in Madagascar for a long time, but the French transferred it to some other place. Now they regret this, and have brought the legion back, because it required so large a force of ordinary troops to cope with the natives. The foreign legion alone could deal with them. I suppose it dealt harshly and savagely with the natives, killing, robbing them, and burning their villages for every offence, real or imaginary. Owing to this the settlements were peaceful, and dared not rise against the French.

January 10th.—In the wardroom of the *Suvaroff* there is a piano on which they play with the help of a pianola. There are very few who play the piano. To-day a sub-lieutenant came on board from another ship. He proved to be a splendid musician. For a long time they listened to his playing. Then they started capering and playing tricks. It was curious to see officers dancing the cake walk and the Kamarinsky (a Russian national dance), etc. They dressed up for these dances. They did this from sheer boredom. This wearisome and monotonous cruise has lasted so long. On the 16th the fleet will have been kicking their heels here for a month. No wonder they are silly from stagnation. Here is another of their amusements—they bait the dogs, and every one eagerly watches, applauding the fighting curs.

There are many suspicious characters in Madagascar. One appeared at Nosi Be, speaking Russian. He offered his services as contractor to supply provisions for the *Suvaroff* and other ships. This person roamed about in Tamatave, and now without any apparent cause has come here. He is very badly dressed and has long hair like a Slav woman.

The mail-steamer left to-night for Europe. From Mayung cipher telegrams have been received. Perhaps they again tell us nothing useful. The situation of the fleet is most unsettled. Will it return to Russia, will it remain somewhere here, or will it go to the East ? No one knows. This uncertainty oppresses me as well as others.

Bad meat is daily thrown overboard in the *Esperanza*. Food for the sharks is abundant. They have collected in great numbers at Nosi Be. Nearly all the ships keep oxen on deck. There is even a cow and a calf on board the *Suvaroff*. They have built them a manger. The crew look after them with special fondness, feeding them with bread and giving them names.

It is a curious sight, watching these animals being brought on board. They come tied up in boats, and are generally hoisted into the ship by means of a strop (loop of rope) tied under their bodies. For some reason, on board the *Suvaroff* they are dragged up by the horns. The frightened animals, with wild and glaring eyes, struggle violently, hanging in mid-air. They lie down on deck at first, half crazy, and then suddenly jump on their feet and toss themselves about. They are then held and pacified.

It was quite different with the cow. She tore herself loose and galloped frantically about the deck. All the spectators fled wherever they could. She charged at the deck-house, where an officer was sitting writing. He had hardly time to shut and lock the door. Somehow or other they caught the cow, but her milk supply has ceased, owing to fright, and the calf is still young. They now feed him on condensed milk. We wonder if the milk will come back to the cow. We are all interested in the matter, and discuss it freely. Life on board is so dreary, dull, and monotonous, that the most paltry trifles, which we would never dream of talking about on shore, become a ceaseless topic of conversation. If we only could get quickly out of this mire!

January 11th.—Heat, stuffiness, damp, dirt—everywhere beastliness, deadly gloom, uncertainty of the near future, lack of news from the seat of war, oppress and overwhelm us; but can incompetence reigning everywhere, laziness, stupidity, ignorance, unwillingness to work, listlessness, make us cheerful? What goes on here is perfectly incredible.

There is news that the Hamburg-American liner *Bengal* sank near the southern coast of Madagascar, having ripped her bottom on a sunken rock. She was a large 18,000-ton steamer, and was bringing coal for the fleet. Her crew were saved.

A deplorably sad and stupid incident occurred in the *Nachimoff* yesterday. Ships having no bakery on board obtain their bread, when at anchorage, from other ships or from the shore. They did not trouble about the matter in the *Nachimoff*. The crew were living on rusks. Yesterday they demanded fresh bread. The affair spread, and the men offered passive resistance by not dismissing after prayers, though ordered to do so. There is now to be an inquiry. At other times and under other conditions some of the crew would have been distributed among the other ships, and some would have been shot—there would have been no other alternative. Now they are trying to hush the matter up. In spite of this, some will suffer.

One of the *Malay* prisoners who was in cells in the *Alexander* has been sent to the hospital-ship *Orel*, as he fell ill from the hot temperature in his prison.

CHAPTER VI

WAITING FOR ORDERS

January 12th.—It is very possible that on the 16th the fleet will receive instructions from Petersburg either to return, proceed to the East, or stay somewhere here until further orders. I wish they would decide quickly. Uncertainty is worse than anything. It is very unhealthy, staying here during the rainy season. Fevers, dysentery, and similar delights are rampant. Europeans cannot stand the climate. Anchorages like our present one end by having a bad effect on the spirits of the crew. They deteriorate. The affair in the *Nachimoff* serves as an example of this.

There has been a signal that we are to have steam up at 6.30 to-morrow morning, in order to go out to sea for firing. This will be our first practice since leaving Revel.

I have not been ashore to-day. I was lazy, though the weather was tolerable. The rain is

A LIVELY OCCUPATION

not incessant. They have brought a puppy on board, some shellfish, and some hermit crabs. They torment the molluscs by pouring eau de Cologne over them, puffing tobacco-smoke at them, and by burning them with matches. A lively occupation, but really it is excusable; there are no distractions, and they have invented this.

January 13th.—Weather is pleasant in harbour; probably it will be calm at sea as well. We are going to fire. We weighed anchor at 8 a.m. French torpedo-boats have followed us. They brought telegrams from Mayung. They went into harbour at Nosi Be, and handed over telegrams to the torpedo-boat *Bodry*. The latter pursued the *Suvaroff*, and passed the telegrams to the admiral by means of a rope-end. What news do they contain?

Firing is just beginning. Everything is tightly closed. The mirrors have been taken down and crockery put away.

6 p.m.—The ships have finished their firing, and we are now going into the anchorage.

Reuter's telegrams state that Petersburg and Moscow are under martial law and surrounded by a chain of troops; that the mutiny of sailors at Sevastopol continues; that they have burnt the barracks and Admiralty there; that the troops have refused to fire on the mutineers; and that military disorders are rife throughout Russia. These telegrams must be read with reserve, but I, at any rate, believe them. During manœuvres to-day the *Borodino* and *Alexander* nearly collided. Thank God, this accident was averted. It would have been appalling.

A few days ago they were doing some work in the *Suvaroff* and opened a valve. They forgot to shut it, and opened another one yesterday, not knowing that the first had not been closed. In the night a whole compartment was flooded, and water poured into the engine-room. How I cursed that I had come in the fleet! Here you sit chained, seeing the mistakes of others, and are powerless to do anything. At times I really fear that I shall go mad.

January 14th.—The colliers brought news that the *Oleg* has captured a steamer which was taking two hundred and sixty field-guns to Japan. It sounds improbable. This steamer, as far as I know, should have gone round Africa; and there our auxiliary cruisers awaited her.

I went to a café on shore and played cards. I lost 170 francs (about 64 roubles). Returned on board about seven o'clock, late for dinner, so dined in my cabin. On shore I saw the man who was suspected of being a spy. He is very like a Russian, and wears his long red hair like an artist.

11 p.m.—Wonderfully practical folk, the Germans! They have sent officers to the colliers to help the captains. These officers are sent in order that they may watch our cruise and give useful information to their own navy. Would Russia do anything similar? No, never! This is why we are paying so dearly now. We are still far from having a fine navy or army. It is not a question of soldiers, but of organising a campaign, of constant preparation and of foresight.

What a variety of coinage there was on the card-table—French, English, Russian, Italian, and Austrian. They play for very high stakes. One lieutenant in an hour won and lost 5,000 francs.

We are daily expecting the arrival of the *Oleg*, *Isumrud*, and torpedo-boats. Judging by time, they are near Nosi Be. This is according to telegraphic agencies. Official news we never receive It is always like that with us in Russia.

The mail-steamer from Europe arrives on the 20th and returns on the 24th. We shall evidently wait here for her.

The supposition that we should remain a long time in Madagascar is amply justified. It is exactly a month to-morrow since the fleet arrived at this island. That is how time flies. We have lost a whole month uselessly, and it is still unknown how much longer we shall be here.

What are they thinking of in Petersburg ? There are rumours here that after Klado's articles the public will demand the return of the fleet to Russia. Can it be that, even now, they are unable to decide whether to go backward or forward ? The upkeep of the fleet costs large sums. It cannot become better or stronger, remaining whole weeks at anchor in Nosi Be. On the contrary, it will do nothing but harm. By wasting time here we give the Japanese the chance of repairing their ships and boilers. They are secretly preparing to meet us now. We have no bases. Can we be trusting to our country or merely to luck ? What were they thinking about in sending the fleet ? Our fleet is Russia's last might. If it is destroyed, we shall have no navy. Every one thinks this—I am not the only one. All this can scarcely raise the spirits of the men. Probably something similar is going on in the army. It is bad ! Everything is bad, and there are internal disorders as well. How will it all end ?

January 15th.—I have again been on shore. I learnt that the steamer *Vladimir* of the volunteer fleet is leaking. I will go and look at her to-morrow. A new signboard has appeared on shore—" Skopolites, contractor of the fleet," in freshly painted characters.

Shortly before leaving the ship a sailor fell into the water and made for a native boat. The negro hawkers took five francs from him, and wanted to row away without him. The sailor was rescued and the negroes were deprived of his money. The officers buy all sorts of useless rubbish, which, after they have taken it on board, is thrown aside and forgotten. I posted a letter to-day, went to the café, and played macao, winning 250 francs. I went round the shops, but, finding nothing of interest, returned to the café. I did not play, and afterwards set out for the quay.

The *Esperanza* has just come from sea. She leaves the harbour daily to throw bad meat overboard. She informs us that she saw three large warships and one small one far away. Perhaps they are Japanese. I myself saw a Japanese on shore to-day. Many others saw him. At one time there were not any to be seen.

Cipher telegrams have again been received.

They have not yet been deciphered. It is astonishing that they should inform us in cipher who has received rewards. The telegraphic agencies relate horrors about Russia's internal affairs. Among other things they mention serious disorders in Petersburg. They say that it has come to barricades in the street—that more than 2,000 men are killed, and more than 7,000 wounded. I fancy they lie, but there is never smoke without fire.

I have to go to the hospital-ship *Orel* to-morrow. The boats have to be fitted for the transport of the wounded. What were they thinking of before? This steamer was fitted out as a hospital and cost a great deal of money, but the boats were forgotten. Everywhere we make some stupid mistake.

My beard has grown tremendously, and is very shaggy. I have not trimmed it. Every one hinted that it was time to have it cut, and at last the admiral and flag-captain spoke about it. I summoned the sailor Michael, who cut it so short that, looking in the glass, I did not recognise myself.

January 16th.—The *Esperanza's* news has produced active measures. Until the moon rises all fighting-lamps are to be lit. They had seen that the Japanese, whom I mentioned yesterday, was sending telegrams by heliograph. He attempted to come on board our ships with the contractors.

The German colliers brought news that newly bought ships are coming to reinforce us, and are at present at Cape Verde. Probably this is another canard. We shall soon see if it is true. It is a month's voyage for them to Nosi Be. This reinforcement would be most welcome. I do not believe in it. These same Germans assure us that the Black Sea fleet has left. They spoke about this long ago, and there is no sign of it. They evidently mistook the *Oleg* and her companions for the Black Sea fleet.

I have been on board the *Keiff* and *Vladimir* of the volunteer fleet to-day. Life in them is heavenly compared with life on board ships of the *Borodino* type. There is plenty of space and the cabins are large, clean, and quiet. They live well, have free communication with the shore, etc. I remained to lunch in the *Vladimir*, and returned to my ship in her steamboat.

Some sailor in the transport *Jupiter* out of revenge cast off the collier's boat from the steamer and it drifted ashore with the current. Although it was night and the boat was floating away from the transport, they managed to catch it.

There is a church on shore. Many Roman Catholics took the opportunity of making their confession. The confession was an empty one— that is, they did not confess to a priest, as the greater part of them had not command enough of the French language to speak of their sins.

My servant brought me a letter to be sent to his wife. "My wife," he said, "is also called Sophie." He is a curious fellow, but I am satisfied with him.

I heard various details of the Petersburg disorders in the *Vladimir*.

The Europeans here live in a most extraordinary way. They come to the colony to make money, and then quickly return to their own countries. They deprive themselves of everything. They live almost in huts, and do not spend a sou more than they can help. After a few years of such life they become fairly well off, and leave the colony for ever. Their abodes are like a camp. The furniture is bad and broken. There are no conveniences, and no thought of comfort.

There is no news. Telegrams are sent by heliograph to Diego Suarez.

January 17th.—A telegram has been received saying the *Rezvy* has left her division, and remains at Jibutil owing to breakdown. She will probably not go to the East at all.

Yesterday the local governor came to the admiral with a complaint that the officers of the fleet play games of hazard for high stakes at the café. Play is forbidden or all leave will be stopped. Two or three days ago the German colliers celebrated Wilhelm's birthday. They dressed their ship with flags and drank so much that they remained drunk until to-day.

As the fleet moves forward the number of torpedo-boats grows less and less. Those that remain with us have damaged boilers, thanks to which they are unable to attain their full speed.

The captain of the port at Diego Suarez went round our ships. He was saluted. Evidently this amused him.

To-morrow part of the fleet are going to sea for target-practice.

When shall we leave here? We are losing the best weather. Hurricanes, cyclones, and storms will begin soon, and with a fleet like ours the voyage will be very difficult. Before us lies an immense passage—viz. from Madagascar to the islands of the East Indian Archipelago.

January 18th.—Owing to high play we are forbidden to go ashore on weekdays. An order has been given to verify the cash of all the paymasters in the fleet.

The inhabitants of Nosi Be consider the fleet the cause of there being so little rain. It generally comes down in bucketfuls every day during the rainy season. Now the rain is coming at intervals and it is bad for the crops. The natives are making offerings and have started a religious procession. Perhaps they are right, and the fleet is the cause of so little rain. It is necessary for the downpour of tropical rain that much electricity should collect in the air. It may be that the masts of our ships conduct the current of electricity into the water, not allowing it to collect in sufficient quantities in the air for rain. Doubtless the natives explain it differently.

More and more frequently, at times, there falls on me complete oblivion to my surroundings. I have become absolutely apathetic. Everything is quite indistinct. Nothing interests me. My mind is crushed. I have such attacks of endless despair, such fancies, such horrible thoughts, that, by God, I do not know what to do, where to hide, or how to forget myself.

8 p.m.—We have returned and anchored at

Nosi Be. To-morrow the fleet must go to sea again for firing.

Since this morning they have been painting my cabin. How am I to sleep? It smells strongly of paint and turpentine. It will most probably give me a headache.

The French torpedo-boats have brought neither telegrams nor news to-day. I got up early this morning and had no rest during the day, am fearfully tired, and shall have to get up earlier than ever.

January 19*th*.—Since communication with the shore is forbidden, I have to take every opportunity of sending my letters. I think it will be difficult for you to read my epistles. They are full of broken, unconnected sentences and muddled incidents. It will most likely be difficult for me to make them out myself. You receive several at a time, and that makes it more confused.

Up till 8 a.m. we were getting up anchor, and then we went out to sea. Yesterday a projectile ricochetted on to the *Donskoi*. It touched the bridge, slightly damaged it, and flew further. No one was killed or wounded, thank God! It might have had a much worse ending.

At five o'clock we returned to Nosi Be, not having hit anything this time.

The admiral received a letter from the individual whom they suspected of being a spy, in which he complains of the unjust accusation. He says that an officer tried to poison him when he went on board the *Ural*, and that the Governor has offered to send him away from Nosi Be. Finally, he begs for money for his passage. The contractor with whom he came on board explained to the Governor about him. Among other things the contractor says that the man is continually disappearing, that they had to look for him in the ship, and that once he ate from the common tub with the crew. Knowing Russian, he was able to hide from the officers.

Is it not extraordinary? A spy is going about our ships quite unpunished. It is a marvel! As if anything similar could happen to the Japanese! I do not think so! It is all so disgusting that I do not like to speak of it. You know what sort of characters there are in the fleet. When we were in Russia a man came and begged to be allowed to join the fleet. He threatened that if they did not take him he would shoot himself, and appointed a time. They accepted him, promoted him to the rank of petty officer, and then discovered that he was under age. However, it was too late; he is now cruising. There are several indications that the fleet will not leave here soon.

They have brought news from the shore that Kuropatkin is about to take the initiative. We have already heard this so many times that we do not believe it.

January 20th.—To-day the French mail-boat ought to arrive. Many expect letters. Communication with the shore is allowed. I do not want to go, and have asked some officers to buy me three mats, three caps, and some postage stamps. I do not understand how they can go ashore just as the mail will be brought on board and be sorted. Do they really not care for the letters or for their contents? No; evidently "we are not all made of the same dough." Force would not take me out of the ship just now. It may be that the post we expected to receive from the *Oleg* has just been brought by the French mail-steamer.

What a disappointment! Only boots and tobacco, which were ordered and not sent to Admiral Folkersham through lack of time.

They brought the mail to the *Suvaroff* and began sorting it. I took an active part, cutting the bags, sorting the letters, and calling out the names of the ships. A great many officers helped. Writers came from all the ships, and surrounded the deck-house where the letters were being sorted. Sometimes a letter for me fell into my hands. I put it into my pocket. Sometimes my name was called out and a letter given me.

The sorting ended, I flew to my cabin, and there on the table was another letter and a large official parcel. The latter was a book on ship-construction sent by the Committee. The rest of the letters were from you. I read them, and did not know what to do. I was agitated. I went and sat in an armchair in the admiral's after-cabin, and gazed and gazed through the balcony door at the harbour.

An orderly came and said that a cadet from the *Borodino* was asking for me. I was surprised. I went out, and he gave me another packet of letters bound with a ribbon, and said his captain found them among his letters. I thanked the cadet, and begged him to express my thanks to the captain. To whom were not letters addressed? To those ships lying quietly at Libau and Cronstadt, and to the ships that had been destroyed at Port Arthur. There was a letter for Popoff, who was killed in the *Ural*, and one for Titoff, who went mad and is in the *Malay*. Every one, having read their letters, seized the papers and devoured them greedily, grew heated, and quarrelled.

Dinner to-day was specially lively. Several of the staff received rewards. Everybody had letters and parcels, and, what was extraordinary, most of the parcels contained warm clothing. There were many toasts drunk, and the band played. Two fellows were moved to tears. They had not had news from home for a long time, and now they received it all at once. If a torpedo-boat brings me your telegram, I shall be quite happy.

January 21*st*.—A Japanese spy came on board the *Suvaroff* yesterday in the guise of a trader. No attempt, even, was made to detain him. The officials at the post-office are surprised that the Russians send all their letters registered.

From the post-office I went round the shops with an officer. I bought some lovely postcards. We wandered into the village. A dog that was with us had a slight sunstroke. We took it into a café, rubbed its head with ice, bathed it, and now it has recovered.

There is news that order has been established in Petersburg. Thank God! The French say that the *Oleg* only left Jibutil on the 20th. That means she will not be here for a week.

They have just read aloud in the wardroom the answer from Admiral Birilieff. As you can imagine, the majority are furious with him. They say, "How dare he abuse the fleet? Who gave him the right to do so? He knows nothing about it, though he is serving in the navy." These naval men dare to talk, after having ignominiously and needlessly ruined a navy twice as strong as the Japanese, scarcely doing any harm to the latter.

What can be more infamous than the conduct of our navy? There has been nothing like it since the creation of the world. Words fail me to describe the shameless dishonour. They have the impertinence to say, "Who dare criticise us?" Imagine what I heard to-day. They said, "What the devil does it mean? It is perfectly revolting! Rewards are showered on the land forces, and we sailors have had nothing for Port Arthur." I am telling you the truth, word for word. When I heard it I was thunderstruck.

When will there be an end to this inefficiency, bragging, and conceit? Russia may not ask these officers, "Where is the navy that was built by the sweat of millions of Russian people? What has it done? Has it done harm to the enemy? Will it help the fatherland? Will it add to the glory of

Russia ? " Oh no ! you must not ask sailors these questions. They are more expert engineers than engineers themselves. They have more legal knowledge than lawyers. The naval ministry was created for themselves. They are demi-gods. They only are entitled to honours, riches, glory, everything; but naval work they do not understand. They do not serve for war, and are not prepared for it. The navy is to them the means of getting all the good things of life. They may be judges of others, hold their heads high and say, " We are naval officers. What more do you want ? "

However bitter this may sound, it is true. Do you remember my telling you how it would be ? This voyage confirms my old opinions. To think that Russia counts on them ! I never cared for Birilieff as a man, but we must thank him and Klado for their articles. Let Russia make acquaintance with the archaic systems of, and what she can expect from, our glorious Russian navy.

I was getting ready for church just as they brought me your telegram. I was tremendously pleased, and no wonder, as I was waiting nine days for my answer.

They are sending the band to play on the shore. The officers played tennis with the governor and his wife. A sad thing happened on shore: a sailor hit a petty officer in the face.

January 24th.—Thanks to the affair yesterday, leave to go ashore is only granted for the half-day. If it is absolutely necessary to send a boat later, then they have to ask the admiral's permission.

It appears that there were several disturbances on shore yesterday, and all caused by a petty officer.

To-morrow we are going to sea for target-practice. To-day the torpedo-boat *Blestyastchy* (Brilliant) lowered a boat, which capsized. Three men were drowned. There are fatalities in the fleet nearly every day.

January 25th.—I read the newspaper cuttings you sent me. While the ships went out for target-practice, the mining cutters were left behind for exercise. They went a little way out to sea, and saved six natives whose catamaran upset.

One officer had sunstroke, but recovered. It is very dangerous to go about here with an uncovered head, or to take off one's cap frequently, even if the sun is behind clouds. The Europeans do not risk going out of doors without a helmet. They continually warn Russians, but we are like the man who does not cross himself when it is not thundering.

Perhaps we shall go to sea to-morrow for evolutions and firing. On Sunday it is proposed to have a race for the boats of all ships in the fleet. Many are grumbling—they will not be able to go ashore owing to these races.

What a lot of time the fleet has wasted lying here! We might have been at Vladivostok by now. The *Oleg* is detained somewhere. She will arrive at the end of the month. I think with horror that, even with her arrival, in Petersburg they have not yet decided our fate, but compel us to wait for the third fleet. And when will it reach here! Not for a long time—not for a very long time.

January 26th.—When I was in the wardroom on board the *Aurora* a cannon-shot suddenly thundered overhead. It was the *Kamchatka* saluting the corpse of the sailor who died in the hospital-ship *Orel*. Passing the *Kamchatka*, with white foam at her bows, was a long, narrow, black torpedo-boat. A row of men dressed all in white stood on her deck. The sound of the funeral hymn was heard. In the stern stood the priest with incense, near the coffin, which was sewn up with yellow canvas and covered with St. Andrew's flag.[1] The torpedo-boat was

[1] The Russian naval flag is white, with a blue St. Andrew's cross on it.

carrying out to sea for burial another Russian, who had died far from home. Many have perished in the fleet. Not long ago three men were drowned. Another one has died to-day. I am told that during the evolutions of the fleet the *Suvaroff* nearly rammed the *Kuban*.

January 26th.—It is exactly a year to-day since the war with Japan began. A sad anniversary! Up to now this war has brought us nothing but shame, misfortune, and ruin.

The *Svietlana* was told to bring the Russian mail from Mojanga. We received it at six o'clock. There is again a mix-up of addresses. Letters were addressed to the Electrotechnical Institute of the Emperor Alexander III.

January 29th.—A curious comedy has been enacted on shore by the Governor's wife and the wife of a merchant. The Governor's wife came to the other lady and accused her of spreading scandal, saying that the Governor had complained to Admiral Rojdestvensky that the Russian officers were getting drunk on shore. "My husband," said the Governor's wife, "did not go to the admiral; but your husband went to complain that the officers were behaving badly. I know why he did it. The officers did not get drunk, but they paid you attentions and you encouraged them. It is owing to you that the officers are not allowed on shore," etc.

The ladies were thoroughly frightened. The merchant has now written to the flag-captain, stating this story and asking for "satisfaction," as he never complained, and, on the contrary, could not praise enough the behaviour of the officers. (I told you why their leave was stopped—it was owing to their gambling at cards.) It would be interesting to know how the flag-captain answered the merchant, and what the latter will do with the "satisfaction" if he gets it. Again it is a case of women.

I wanted to seal a parcel, and remembered that they do not accept them with seals at the post-office, as sealing-wax melts from the heat.

It is difficult to understand how the traders make a living here. They have opened several shops and raised the prices tremendously. They intrigue against each other and complain to the admiral. The *Esperanza* bought up all the provisions at Mojanga, and has now gone for materials. What a quantity of money the ships have spent here! Truly Russia has enriched Nosi Be, Mojanga, and Diego Suarez. They have even ordered goods from France.

January 30th.—It is very hot to-day. It is long

since there were heavy rains. Light rain does not cool the sides of the ship, which remain hot the whole twenty-four hours.

Lunch to-day was interrupted by the funeral of a sailor of the *Borodino*. The torpedo-boat passed the *Suvaroff* with his body. The man died in a very strange way. He was in the hospital-ship *Orel*. He was discharged from the sick-list, and was sitting waiting for the boat to take him back to the *Borodino* when he fell down dead. Behind the torpedo-boat came a steamboat with the captain. He was accompanying his sailor to burial.

The majority of officers have leave to go ashore to-day until 6 p.m. The watches of a good number are damaged, broken, or choked with dust. They have bought up all the watches in the place, and many of these are broken and cannot be mended. They have cleared everything out of Mojanga. At the bank they cannot even change a credit note for a few thousand francs.

A good many people earn a living as money-changers. For a pound they sometimes give 24 francs 50 centimes, and sometimes 25 francs 40 centimes. Thus on a pound, which is less than ten roubles, you lose about 34 copecks (8*d*.). The fleet is paid in pounds, and loses considerably. A

German company here buys up all the pounds and gains large profits. The officers want to ask them to change the credit notes.

This is how the Germans do business. They buy land and let it to ruined Frenchmen, compelling them to sell vanilla at a low price. They buy up leather, cocoa-nut oil, coffee, etc., and send it green to Europe, where it is sold at immense profit.

They say that when the band played on shore to-day the local queen was present. She is of no importance, and has been left alone by the French, who are the real owners of the country. This queen behaves with dignity, and does not ask for money.

A sailor in the *Oslyabya* stole a box of church offerings. He was found out and arrested, and will probably be tried by special court.

January 31st.—I went ashore at 10 a.m. I went to a vanilla plantation, called at the church and at the school, which is kept by the Carmelite order. I am sitting in a restaurant with an officer. We are drinking lemonade with grenadines and ice in it. By twelve I shall be on board the *Suvaroff*, and at one attend a court of inquiry. At the plantation we had an argument with some Frenchmen because we had broken a branch of vanilla. The heat was so great that I drank plain water, which I never do on shore. It is extraordinary how spoilt the natives are. They followed us all the time, although we drove them off, and then demanded a tip.

February 4th.—There has been a dreadful storm. The lightning was blinding and the thunder absolutely deafening. Russian sign-boards are hung all over Nosi Be. Among them is the following: "Tremendous bargains! Come and buy."

There is a dearth of stamps in the post-office. For a long time there have been no 25-centime stamps, and very few of any other kind.

February 5th.—The admiral has been unwell lately. He had neuralgia so badly yesterday that he even moaned. He did not sleep last night, and is now lying down. He does not listen to the doctor's advice. He did not come to morning tea or lunch.

I had my hair cut and my beard trimmed. Do you know how this operation is performed? The flagship's barber Michael appears in dirty working clothes, with a box in which are a machine, an old brush, and a razor. You sit on a chair and cover yourself with a towel. Michael cuts. It is hot, and the perspiration drops from his face. Having finished, he puts up his implements, receives a copper, shakes out the towel, hangs it up, gathers up from the deck the fallen hairs, presses them into his fist, and departs. All this is done so simply.

The admiral did not leave his cabin even for meals to-day. The doctors now say that he has rheumatism. Last night he cried out with pain. They wanted some ice for him. There was none in the *Suvaroff*, so an officer went to the other ships to find some. The confusion was great.

February 6th.—As the admiral is ill I did not get up for breakfast. Woke just before nine and went to sleep again until five o'clock. It was not very hot and stuffy. Usually it is impossible to sleep by day in a cabin.

There was mass to-day.

A Frenchman who has opened a shop on shore came to tell us about a Japanese spy. We do not believe him, and think he is making a report to advertise his wares. As a rule Frenchmen are great humbugs. The admiral recovered and came to dinner. Some of the officials at the post-office have learnt Russian words. They show off their knowledge by writing "Petersburg" on the receipts in Russian.

We still remain here, and Nosi Be is getting quite Russianised. From the telegrams which the French torpedo-boat brought from Mojanga we learn that the Governor-General of Moscow has been killed, and that the third fleet left Libau on February 2nd.

It will be a surprise if we are obliged to wait for the famous third fleet. It is very injurious for our ships, being kept in Nosi Be. Their underwater parts will be covered with barnacles and waterweeds (commonly known as beard). Owing to this ships steam considerably slower and require a greater expenditure of coal, etc. The barnacles and beard have to be cleaned off in dock, and there are none available in this part of the world. Cleaning the underwater parts with the help of divers is slow and unsatisfactory. How important it is may be seen from the fact that even merchant ships voyaging in southern and eastern waters go into dock to be cleaned at least once in six months. We shall arrive in the East with dirty ships, and the Japanese will meet us in clean ones. Our ships will have just made a long voyage, and theirs will come out of harbour.

Another fine thing is that the Japanese will raise our ships sunk at Port Arthur, repair them, and oppose them to us under their old names. They will strengthen their fleet in this way, and what a disgrace it will be for Russia. Imagine the scene! Some *Poltava* or *Retvizan* will fire on the *Suvaroff*. It is too disgusting to think of! And who is it who has annihilated the fleet? The Japs—" Apes," as our gallant sailors call them! Such self-confidence, conceit, and contempt for the monkey Japs will cost Russia dearly. Here I go again, harping on the old tune. I had better stop, as it does not help.

February 7th.—I lunched in the battleship *Orel*. Had soup with rice—and caterpillars. A satisfying meal, was it not? The officers of the *Orel* are convinced that for several evenings running they have seen a balloon on the horizon signalling with lights. One of the officers thought of ordering himself a pair of white trousers made out of a sheet, as material is not to be had. There is a consoling description of the *Cesarevitch's* damages. Fifteen twelve-inch shells struck her (this is a tremendous number, and twelve-inch shells are the heaviest), and not one pierced her armour. Our battleships *Suvaroff*, *Borodino*, *Alexander*, and *Orel* are better armoured than the *Cesarevitch*. If twelve-inch shells could not pierce her armour, smaller projectiles can do almost nothing—that is, if they hit protected parts. Some of the eye-witnesses in the *Rossia* and *Gromoboi* say that the first impressions of the battle were horrible. Everything was upside-down and broken to bits. You looked round and saw that nothing that was behind armour was touched, and no substantial damage done to the ship. All this is very nice, but an endless stay at Nosi Be deprives one of all energy.

February 8th.—I have been to the *Anadir*, *Kamchatka*, and to the shore. I went to the cemetery. The caretaker showed me the grave of a Japanese. I told him to put Popoff's grave in order, as it had fallen in.

February 9th.—A " tragic occurrence " took place in the *Suvaroff* to-day. Some one had eaten a monkey. There remained only a bit of tail and a piece of skin. This is the work of either rats or dogs.

I called at a torpedo-boat this morning. The captain and officer were sitting on deck drinking tea. Both were barefooted and in vests and white trousers. I cannot get accustomed to such a sight, somehow. The captain's left foot astonished me. It had only one toe. All the rest had been torn off long ago. The sight of it gave me a queer feeling.

To-day there was a court-martial on an officer. In defence of another officer he had written a report in a very insolent manner to the captain. By order of the admiral the officer was dismissed from the *Ural* in January, and now he is placed on the retired list by the general staff. I do not know how the trial will end. They say he is a very good fellow. The offence of which he is accused is very seriously punished—either by degradation to the rank of sailor or confinement in a fortress.

February 10th.—The court sentenced the officer to be dismissed the service and deprivation of rank. The sentence will go to the admiral for confirmation. The punishment imposed by the court is the lightest possible. It came out that there is much slackness in the *Ural*. The matter will hardly end here, as they say K—— is an obstinate man, and will raise it again in Petersburg.

There has just been a storm in a tea-cup. Smoke appeared from a cabin. They manned the pumps and nearly rang the fire alarm. It was discovered that a white tunic lying in a basket had caught fire. They pulled out the basket, drew out the tunic, and the panic subsided.

The meat at dinner to-day was bad. I ate a good deal before I discovered what was the matter.

I am trying to find a tortoise on shore. If I find one, I shall keep its shell for combs and hairpins for you.

From several sources news has been received that there are Japanese ships near Madagascar. The Japanese would hardly be so stupid as to split up their fleet. Things have come to such a pass in our ships that they are positively certain that the fleet will return to Russia on March 15th. They told me this in the *Nachimoff,* announcing this sensational news as the latest trustworthy information. I stayed a long time in the wardroom of the *Nachimoff,* talking to an engineer whom I had known at school.

Four sailors of the torpedo-boat *Grosny* (Menacing) broke into a hut and stole the contents. They were caught. There will be a trial, and they will be severely punished. Is it worth it? The damage is assessed by the negroes at sixty francs, all told. The men will be ruined for a mere trifle.

The heat is dreadful! You "stew in your own juice," as they say here, and you drink without ceasing. It is a good thing that the refrigerator in the *Suvaroff* is repaired and you can have ice. At the present moment I have a glass of iced water by me. It cannot be had by all. When the refrigerator was not working they obtained ice for the admiral from other ships. You cannot imagine the delight of drinking something cold, if you have not experienced such great heat. They make a good deal of ice artificially in the fleet, and on shore they trade in it.

I have heard there are cigarettes in the *Tamboff*: I must go and get some.

February 12th.—Under cover of the French newspapers they are talking about the conclusion of peace. They begin to say that it must be concluded, come what may—even to paying a large indemnity. Has Russia really come to this ? Is the war really lost ? I cannot bear to think so ! The disgrace was already bad enough, but what a shameful ending ! Unhappy times ! Everything is going badly, both at the war and in the interior of Russia. How will it all end ?

They say that in the *Tamboff* cigarettes are being sold at fifteen roubles a hundred. It is very dear, but there is nothing to be done. I shall be glad if I can get some, even at that price.

Several cases of champagne were brought to the *Suvaroff* to-day. Some sailors managed to conceal one and hid it in the furnace of a boiler. They were caught. If the matter is officially dealt with, they will suffer severely.

February 14th.—I sent a telegram to you yesterday. There are many sailors who have not been on shore since we left Cronstadt. A large number were last on shore at Revel. A short time ago a sailor of the *Kamchatka* took two lifebelts, jumped overboard at night, and struck out for the shore. He was seen by chance while swimming. The searchlight was turned on to him. " I was tired of being on board, could endure it no longer, and wanted to go on shore," he said in his defence. I quite understood the man's feelings. I am much astonished at many of the officers. They have not been on dry land since they left Revel, although they have had opportunities of leaving the 'ship.

My spirits are depressed. Nothing is known as to when our wanderings will end. I am ready to do almost anything—even to leaving the fleet, which perhaps will not go to the East until the war is over. How I curse myself for having come! Do you know there are forty-two ships at Nosi Be under the Russian naval and merchant flags? A solid figure, but how many are only transports? How many officers and men, do you suppose? I fancy considerably more than 12,000.

CHAPTER VII

EVENTS AT NOSI BE

FEBRUARY 15*th*.—I must without fail go on shore to-day after dinner to post my letters. I do not trust others.

I saw a wedding of a mulatto and a Malagassy. A long procession of negroes went to the mayor's to sign the contract, and then went to the church, where the priest married them. I looked on at the ceremony. Both were young and dressed like Europeans, and had boots on. The bride wore a veil, white dress, etc. During the marriage service dogs ran about the church, but this did not disturb any one. Probably dogs are not considered unclean animals here.[1] Black boys served the priest. The priest himself was a European missionary. The whole church was full of black worshippers. Of course, there were many of our officers there as spectators. After the service the little Malagassy

[1] In Russia a church has to be re-consecrated after a dog has entered it.

with his wife on his arm walked round among the guests collecting money. I gave them a franc. It seemed strange, seeing a Christian church full of blacks reverently fulfilling Christian rites.

How dreadfully the men drink sometimes! To-day I saw a sailor being carried on a stretcher, unconscious and shaking with spasms. It was a repulsive sight. They say the captain of the *Oleg* is in poor health. If it is consumption, the result will be a sad one. If there is only the suspicion of it, in this climate the end comes quickly. The wardroom have made another acquisition. They have obtained a small crocodile from somewhere. The *Suvaroff* is positively becoming a floating menagerie.

We shall probably leave for the East at the end of the month. If that is the case, why is the third fleet sent? Every one acts as he thinks fit. There are no plans, forethought, or system.

February 16th.—There is anxiety about the fate of the *Irtish*. She was at Port Said on January 9th, and should have been here long ago. They have telegraphed asking about her. It is exactly two months to-day since we came to Madagascar. If we leave Nosi Be and go straight to the East, there will be a great break in my letters and telegrams. Do not be anxious. It is quite normal, as we have before us a voyage which, under favourable conditions, lasts twenty days.

To-day I indulged myself and drank some kvass[1] in the *Aurora*. I stayed there some time. Many officers are sceptical, and do not believe that we shall go to the East.

Wrangles are beginning. Two of the captains of torpedo-boats quarrelled as to where they were to lie for coaling. One of them was so much insulted that he went to the *Suvaroff* in his torpedo-boat to complain. No sooner was this story done than another began. The flagship's torpedo officer, who had a number of monkeys, received an order to rid the ship of these animals (he had a cabin full of them). This order was brought out owing to a report from the senior staff-officer, in whose cabin one of the monkeys had been and made himself at home. They contradicted each other in the flag-captain's cabin, and the story promises to be played out. In the evening an officer of the *Suvaroff* shouted out something to the *Oslyabya*, who did not notice a peace attack of torpedo-boats. In the *Oslyabya* they are anxious to know the name of the officer. There will probably be a complaint to the staff to-morrow.

February 17th.—I do not know how the quarrel

[1] A liquor made of rye flour and malt.

of the torpedo captains has ended. One of them came to the staff to-day with explanations.

February 19*th*.—I have bought myself about 2,000 cigarettes. They are without mouthpieces. The tobacco is black and the taste indifferent. If I cannot get Russian ones I must content myself with these.

I had to go on board the *Borodino* late this evening. It was not very pleasant. Frequently the challenge of the sentries in the ships which we have to pass is not heard, owing to the noise of the water and the steam. They fire instantly if the boat does not give the countersign.

Some telegram from Europe was posted up at the post-office. The Governor ordered it to be taken down, so that Russian officers should not read it. Can it be another terrible misfortune? The telegrams that remained announced that the Japanese had cut off Vladivostok almost completely. There are hardly any war stores in Vladivostok. Four steamers were sent from there to Port Arthur while it was holding out, and all fell into the hands of the Japanese. They are taking the guns from Port Arthur and are fortifying the coast of Korea with them.

Where can our fleet go if Vladivostok is cut off ? Even if we succeed in getting there before it is captured, there are no stores there, and in the fleet there are few. We starving shall come to the famished. The fleet will then perish, as it did at Port Arthur. Do you know that the *Bogatyr* sank while coming out of dock? They were able to place a floating dock under her. The Japanese have sent cruisers and torpedo-boats to Vladivostok. Matters are going badly for Kuropatkin.

Have you heard that Japan and France have concluded the following agreement ? Our fleet can remain at Nosi Be as long as it is convenient, but if it leaves even for only three days, then it shall not have the right to enter a French port for three months.

Yes, it must be admitted the situation of Russia is desperate. There are many things I cannot tell you of on paper. They would not improve the general outlook. The *Esperanza*, which is lying at Mojanga, has prepared to come here four times, and each time her machinery has been damaged. Evidently her crew have done it purposely.

I received your telegram to-day. In it is one word, "Well"; at all events, I know you are alive.

Since the beginning of December our Admiralty has not sent us a single letter.

I went to church to-day. It is the memorial day of those warriors who laid down their lives on the field of battle.

At eleven o'clock I set out for the *Borodino*. I was induced to put on my dirk. I never wear it, but hung it on for this occasion. In going down the ladder I caught it on something. It came out, fell into the water, and sank in twelve fathoms. It is impossible to get it. An engineer in the *Borodino* promised to make me a dummy handle. I shall wear it fastened to the scabbard, so that it will look all right. Of course, a proper dirk is not to be had here.

There was a very grand and gay lunch in the *Borodino*. They decorated the wardroom, covered the deck with carpets, and arranged plants in every corner. They laid the table in the form of the letter π (p), placed flower-pots on them, and scattered flowers on the table-cloth. In front of each place was an illuminated menu. There were many guests. The band played. They are a very happy ship. They are always joking, laughing, and amusing themselves, and yet they never forget their duty.

After lunch had been reduced to fragments, the wine flowed in streams. They stationed the band close to the wardroom. Several officers conducted the band themselves. They played my beloved Little Russian march. At first I drank nothing, but having eaten my fill, and sitting listening to the band and hearing the march, I began to drink champagne. Many were drinking it, and with each glass I remembered how you feared I should take to drink. Several officers began to dance. At six o'clock I returned to my ship.

The mail-steamer *Esperanza* has arrived. There were very few letters for the fleet. There was only one bag, and that was sent by Günsburg (agents). From the newspapers we learn what is going on in Russia, and the orders of our Ministry about killed and wounded, etc. I cannot speak calmly. My anger rises, and I am ready to do God knows what! How I curse myself for having come!

February 23rd.—At last the *Irtish* has been found. She left Jibutil on the 17th, so will be here on the 27th or 28th. If only a mail could be brought by her, but our Ministry would never have thought that they could send letters to Jibutil up to the 17th. From there the *Irtish* could have brought them to the fleet. Although there is little hope of this, I shall await her arrival with impatience.

February 24th.—I have just returned from the harbour. I am very much pleased with the work of the divers in the *Jemchug*; they have carried it out brilliantly. I was rather doubtful of success at first. I asked that a letter should be written to the admiral about the successful work of the officers and divers who took part in it. The captain promised to do so, and I for my part undertook to put in a few words.

Some home-made kvass has made its appearance in the *Suvaroff*. I drink it incessantly. It is indifferent kvass, but at least it is Russian. A boy from the *Borodino*, whose name I do not remember, has just come to ask me to help him gain permission to be examined for the rank of petty officer.

I am preparing myself to go ashore at three o'clock. I shall call at the post-office, walk through the streets, and freshen myself up. The shore at least is a change, however dull it may be.

February 26th.—The Malagassy are beginning to be impertinent in offering their services. Europeans do not stand on much ceremony with them. When they saw me with a parcel in my hands, a crowd rushed to the verandah of the shop. The

European clerk grew angry, jumped up, and kicked them like dogs. It did not disconcert them in the least.

At the post-office I was given telegrams and local letters for the fleet. Among the letters was a postcard for Admiral Rojdestvensky. On it the Germans were jeering at him about the North Sea affair, and advising him to return, " the more so as they have prepared vodky for you." [1]

At three o'clock a wireless message was received from the *Irtish*. At eight she arrived in the harbour. There is scarcely a line in her. The cursed staff have not sent the mail by her, although they might easily have done so. The *Irtish* was lying at Jibutil for nearly a month. How every one abused the staff! Can you wonder at it, when even the chief of the staff himself sends letters to his son by Günsburg. How can we fight Japan when they cannot arrange such a simple matter as sending the mails? We have not received a word from home for two and a half months, thanks to their negligence in not putting two and two together. If they cannot do this much that is absolutely necessary for the moral welfare of the personnel

[1] " They will give you a warm welcome." Vodky is a very strong spirit, drunk everywhere in Russia.

of the fleet, how are they to contend against an enterprising foe like Japan? Knowing their disposition, I little expected to receive anything by the *Irtish*; but others were certain that there would be a very large mail. Their disappointment is very great. The first officer of the *Irtish* went mad, and was sent back to Russia from Suez. I hope to go on board her to-morrow, and must also go to the *Borodino*.

February 27th.—I counted on getting cigarettes in the *Irtish*, but there were none. They required them themselves.

In many ships they have mass on the upper deck. I saw two such services to-day—in the *Oslyabya* and the *Borodino*. I found my way to the latter and remained to lunch. They had pancakes, with smetana.[1] I conversed with the captain a long time, and returned to the *Suvaroff* at two o'clock.

A theatrical troupe has been got up on board the *Borodino*, consisting of ten sailors. They are frequently invited to other ships to give plays.

How they are cursing the General Staff about the mail! In several ships they want to telegraph to the *Novoe Vremya* that the officers

[1] Smetana is sour cream.

request their relations and friends to send their letters through Günsburg's agency at Odessa. Some day I will tell you the part that Günsburg has played in the history of the war. Without him all would have been lost. He provided drink, food, and necessaries for the whole fleet.

News has been received that Mukden has been taken by the Japanese, that the road on the flank of the army has been cut, that we have lost 50,000 killed and wounded and 50,000 prisoners. A fearful catastrophe! At the present condition of affairs the war may be considered lost. We must expect every minute to hear that Vladivostok is either besieged or taken. It is useless for the fleet to go on. Poor Russia, when will your trials be ended? One misfortune brings forth another.

February 28th.—It is creditably asserted that from Europe and America they are taking shells, ammunition, guns, armour, and provisions to Japan, and there are even steamers loaded with only milk. Large flotillas of transports are on their way thither. The Japanese navy and army are furnished in abundance with every necessary. Supplies are procured in an unbroken flow.

Russia is a contrast to Japan. In Manchuria our troops are starving, cold—not clothed, and barefooted; guns and projectiles are scarce. And our fleet—it is ludicrous even to compare it with the Japanese! We are now lying waiting the arrival of Günsburg's steamer *Regina*, which should bring some provisions. One steamer! and our foe has ten!

I am no prophet, but remember my words. In the middle of March Japan will be master of the island of Sagalien, and in April, if not sooner, will besiege Vladivostok, or effect a landing close by. Is it worth while sending our fleet to the East? Let us suppose Vladivostok holds out until our arrival, and that our fleet, after having engaged in battle with the Japanese, reaches it. What then? At Vladivostok there is little coal; there are no shells, powder, or guns; and how many shall we have left after the fight? Again, the Japanese ships after the fight would go to Sasebo, Nagasaki, and other ports; and, quickly repairing their damages, would be ready to fight again. What should we do? At Vladivostok there is only one dock. There are no good workshops, no materials, no workmen. It is quite enough to remember how long they took repairing the *Gromoboi* and *Bogatyr*. Vladivostok will be a second Port Arthur. All this is supposing that Vladivostok can hold out, and that the result of the fight will be the same for us as for the Japanese. It must not be forgotten that we have to go into action with a crew wearied by a tremendous voyage, and that we have to defend our transports, etc.

Perhaps the *Regina* will bring us a mail. We expect her in a few days.

I examined the places in the *Aurora* that were struck by projectiles at the time of the North Sea incident. One of the projectiles turned at nearly a right angle during its destructive flight.

The heat is considerable. How accurately I have calculated the time! I reckoned that on March 1st the fleet would be at Vladivostok. It appears that I was not far wrong. Had it not been for the misfortunes at Port Arthur and on land, we should, according to secret plans, have been approaching Vladivostok on March 1st. In the programme which I worked out in Russia I only made an error of a few days.

In Japan they are hastily finishing the construction of a large cruiser. By the middle of March a large number of gunboats will be prepared, which can be made use of in the Amur river.

I was specially sent for to the *Kamchatka* about her rudder. I thought God knows what had happened, and it turned out to be a trifle. There was a great show in the wardroom in the evening. A rat hunt was organised, and many killed. It is a relaxation from care. For a long time they carried on a successful hunt, in which the ship's dogs took a part.

March 1st.—We might get a mail by the *Regina*, which arrives on the 5th. We have begun active preparations for a very long cruise. It will be very sad if we go without waiting for the mails. In any case, the fleet should wait for the *Regina*. It is impossible to move forward without the provisions which are coming in her. We are evidently not intended to wait for the third fleet. Why do they spend more money for nothing by sending it? If our fleet loses the battle, can the third fleet continue its voyage independently? Even if the battle is indecisive in its results, it is impossible for it to go to the East. A signal has been made fo all ships to be ready to get up anchor in twenty-four hours. The *Regina* has not come yet.

The *Suvaroff* was built in the Baltic shipyard. How often have I looked at her! Sometimes, even, with ill will. Perhaps I had then a presentiment that my fate would be closely bound up with hers.

I will send my letters by a boat going ashore.

I do not know if I shall be able to leave the ship myself. I feel much calmer when my letters are posted. I have made a new reckoning of time. I made out that we can be at Vladivostok in a month and a half after leaving here, if there are no delays on the way. That means that, if nothing happens, and the fleet leaves here soon, we shall see each other at the beginning of May.

March 2nd.—The *Regina* is near. She has entered the harbour and will soon anchor. Possibly we shall weigh anchor to-morrow and go eastward. Do not be anxious that there will be no letters from me for a long time. Under favourable conditions the voyage to the East Indian Archipelago takes three weeks. The *Regina* has brought part of the post. The other part, for some reason, was left at Port Said.

A signal has been made for us to have steam ready by twelve noon, on March 3rd.

I think we shall go from Nosi Be to Saigon. The voyage will be long and wearisome, whatever the weather may be.

There is such hellish heat in my cabin that I am now sitting writing in the after-cabin. People are scribbling in every corner. I can imagine what it will be at the post-office to-morrow. We do not weigh anchor before noon. Before then it will be necessary to post the letters from all the ships of the fleet, and there are more than forty of them. I have finished all my necessary work in the ships in time.

CHAPTER VIII

ACROSS THE INDIAN OCEAN

MARCH 3*rd*.—Leaving Nosi Be ; in the Indian Ocean.

To-day was full of events. This morning I went on shore to send my letters and help dispatch others. There was a large crowd at the post-office. All were hurrying to get rid of their letters by eleven, when there is a cessation of work there until two o'clock. At noon the order was given to be ready to get up anchor. Many people did not succeed in posting valuable packets, parcels, and registered letters. The latter they threw straight into the letter-box, which was instantly filled, and had constantly to be emptied.

I was not looking, and the officer who was with me took my registered letters and put them in the box. I was at that moment putting on stamps for transmission abroad. I was annoyed. I went round the post-office into the back yard, and through a window to a room where they were receiving the letters. I induced a Malagassy to take all the letters out of the box and look for mine, which among the general heap came into my hands. I gave all the letters to a clerk, begging him to send them to Russia registered. I had no time to wait for a receipt. I had to hurry on board. I had the advantage of being known to the clerks—firstly because I had often had business with them, and secondly because I promised them medals and orders. Representations about this are already made. At the post-office they asked me questions like this: "Are you leaving to-day or to-morrow? Are you going straight to Russia from here?" By eleven o'clock I was on board.

It was hard to imagine what was going on this morning on the quay. Everything was quite covered by goods and provisions. Carts with bullocks harnessed to them constantly brought loads. All were hastening with packages to the boats. They were hurriedly closing accounts with the shore.

Lunch passed off quietly, but then came my benefit. Forgive me; I will tell you the rest to-morrow. I am so tired I can scarcely sit. I slept badly last night, and do not feel well. My servant even said. "Look here, your worship, sleep and rest. You have slept very little while at the anchorage, and worked hard." That is true. There has been plenty of work. I shall rest now, if nothing happens to the ships, which God forbid. Here we are, again on our way. The place where we are going is still kept secret.

March 4th.—I must finish my story of yesterday. Soon after lunch news was received from the *Kamchatka* that her condenser did not work. She also reported that a Kingston valve had been torn out, that she was beginning to fill with water, and that they were putting a mat under. I thought they would send me to the *Kamchatka* and keep me there for the whole voyage. I was sent for by the admiral. I went to the *Kamchatka*, and found horror and confusion reigning there. In the engine-room compartment the water was already breast-high. I managed to put it right somehow. It happened that the Kingston was not torn out, but the flap in the Kingston pipe was damaged. They shut the flap, not taking precautionary measures, and ejected it out of the pipe, and water came in through the opening formed. When the danger passed I returned to the *Suvaroff*. The admiral sent me to the *Kamchatka*, to remain until the work was finished.

I went there in the duty steamboat. I sent it back and returned in a rowing-boat to the *Suvaroff*, where another surprise awaited me. They were unable to hoist the steamboat in the *Aurora*. The davits were damaged.

I hastened there. In all the other ships the boats were already hoisted. I set out for the *Aurora* in the admiral's light whaler, which is usually hoisted at the last moment. Every moment was valuable. We had to hurry. The men pulled with all their might. At all costs the *Aurora's* steamboat had to be hoisted, otherwise it would have had to be left behind. The work was strenuous. They hammered, filed, and bound, rove the falls, and the boat was eventually hoisted. I was annoyed at having dirtied myself.

You may imagine the need there was to hurry. All this business began at twelve o'clock, and it was necessary that the fleet should weigh anchor at three o'clock. Weigh anchor! and the *Kamchatka* sinking and a steam-boat not able to be hoisted! Besides this, there was a report from the *Kamchatka* in the morning that there was a breakage in her steering arrangements. I took it on myself to say that she could go with such damages. Nevertheless, I was able to put everything to rights by half-past two. I breathed freely. The signal was hoisted, and we began to get up anchor.

The starting of the fleet was a pretty sight. There were forty-two ships, if you count torpedo-boats and transports. French torpedo-boats came to escort the fleet. They wished us a prosperous voyage, and cheered. Our bands played the Marseillaise. Excitement reigns in the wardroom. Will it be for long? Am I pleased? I cannot understand my own feelings. On one hand I am anxious about the fate of the fleet; on the other, there is the possibility of seeing you soon, and the feeble, feeble hope of beating the Japanese fleet. If by any chance that should happen, Russia will have command of the sea, and the battle-scenes on land will be changed in our favour. If we are beaten—then Japan is strong, very strong.

You know the steamer *Regina* came to us. At the instance of Japan part of the provisions and supplies were unloaded from her at Port Said. How pleased you will be at this! It means that if Japan had wished it, the *Regina* would not have come here at all. We only receive what Japan permits. See what strength this small country exhibits! It is all thanks to her success in the war.

Just imagine the astonishment of Admiral

Nebogatoff's fleet when they learn that we have gone on without waiting for them. In my opinion it is a rash step to divide your forces. It would not have taken much longer waiting for that fleet, as we have already waited two and a half months at Madagascar.

A flag-officer of our staff has received some secret appointment. He remained at Nosi Be, and was advanced two and a half months' pay.

When Lieutenant Radekin was at Diego Suarez the French told him the date of our departure from Nosi Be and of our further course. That was on February 24th. Radekin wrote down the prediction, sealed it, and gave it to me to be opened at sea. Just fancy, the date of our departure was given exactly! The course I cannot verify, as I do not know it myself.

Yesterday, when it grew dark, the ships lit their lights. The sky was brilliant with flashing stars. Forty-five ships! What a grand armada! How difficult it is to direct its movements, and what an enormous extent it occupies! The admiral only left the bridge at nine o'clock. We were then exceedingly hungry, and sat down to dinner. Last evening delays began immediately. The battleship *Orel* reported that some of her machinery was broken. The fleet lessened speed, and the *Orel* steamed with one engine. Something then went wrong with the *Anadir's* machinery. We waited a whole hour while she put it right. To-day all are going successfully. I have noticed that for some reason the tale of damages usually begins at night.

To-day it is gloomy. The sun is not visible. The sea is rather rough. God forbid that we should have bad weather, especially during the first nine days. All the ships are heavily encumbered with coal. There is not a spot on deck free of coal. This has a bad effect on the sea-going qualities of ships.

I lay down to rest, but could not sleep owing to the heat. I forget if I told you I sleep completely uncovered, and keep a small piece of cardboard by me and use it as a fan. Some one has made a bag out of two nets, and is catching fish from the stern gallery. The weather is calm, and a great many fish swim after the ship.

Nearly alongside the *Suvaroff* is the torpedo-boat *Biedovy*.[1] Life in the torpedo-boat is passed on deck. From the ship we can see how they dine and all that is going on.

Yesterday a sailor from the *Kieff* flung himself

[1] This is the torpedo-boat which took the admiral and his staff when the *Suvaroff* sank in the battle of Tsushima.

into the sea and was drowned. What was his mental condition ? Was he afraid that he would be killed. How strange it is ! But I have heard that there are instances when men, fearing to be killed in action, put an end to themselves. Probably the fear of death acts so strongly on these men that they are not themselves. An hour ago a sailor in a fever threw himself overboard from the *Jemchug*. They lowered two whalers and a gig to pick him up, and threw him a life-belt; but he fortunately swam to the hospital-ship *Orel* and climbed on board. Now he is remaining in her.

March 5th (morning).—Last evening something went wrong with the machinery of the transport *Vladimir*. We waited while it was repaired. On the whole we are going very slowly. This morning all the torpedo-boats but one (the duty boat) were taken in tow. This was in order that they should not expend coal, which is very difficult to supply in mid-ocean even when it is comparatively calm. In slightly rough weather it is useless even to think of coaling.

Last evening a German steamer from Diego Suarez, as she explained on being asked, overtook and passed us. This is rather suspicious. Why must she go on the same course as we are going? The route for the fleet was purposely chosen, being one along which no one ever goes. Yesterday the *Navarin* fired to try the carriage of newly placed guns. The sound of the firing reached the *Suvaroff*. This, I thought, is how I shall hear the firing when we meet the Japanese. The sounds are not very loud. Our shots, no doubt, will make more noise.

Slowly, very slowly, we are going ahead. Now and then the fleet stops, and goes on again with a speed of five to eight knots. There are varieties of mishaps, breakages in the *Sissoi*, and in the torpedo-boats *Grosny* and *Gromky*. The slightest damage delays all. Do you know to what distance our ships extend, going in several divisions? Nearly ten versts. If we go on at the same speed we shall expend a great deal of time before reaching any port. We are going north-east, and are again approaching the equator.

The ship scouting reported that she saw a light far away. Perhaps a "chance" vessel, like the one yesterday. In a good cruiser the Japanese might watch every step of our fleet without being perceived by us. We are steaming with lights. What is to prevent a fast cruiser, without lights, from approaching us, ascertaining our position, and disappearing—and no one will ever suspect such observation. If the Japanese do not do that now, it is almost certain that they will watch our fleet when approaching the islands of the East Indian archipelago, in order that, having chosen a favourable time, they may attack, if not the warships, at all events the transports. It is very difficult to defend the latter.

What is Nebogatoff's fleet doing now? Will they really continue their voyage to the East? It will be a great risk.

March 6th (morning).—In the night we remained three hours at one spot. Something was amiss with the steering engine of the *Borodino*. She has not yet put it right, and so is going on the flanks of the rest.

A steamer is coming towards us.

The light which the scouting cruiser saw yesterday, and which she took for a ship, proved to be a star. They say you can often make the mistake, seeing a star setting on the horizon. I saw one like it. Sometimes there is a completely deceptive appearance of a ship's light. It is related that on one occasion, during the last war with Turkey, a whole fleet (in the Black Sea) chased a star. No doubt the mistake was soon found out.

During the cruise life on board passes very monotonously. There are no events except breakages. All are tired of one another. They converse little and about nothing, and sit in different corners. I have not been much in the wardroom lately. I do not play games or the pianola. I sit mostly in the deck-house, on the bridge, or in the flag-captain's cabin.

There was mass to-day. The weather has become a little rougher. We are going desperately slowly so shall not reach a port soon. We have to cross a whole ocean. Another pleasure is in store for the fleet—coaling in the open sea.

Night.—The whole port side of the spar-deck is occupied by oxen and cows. The oxen for meat and the cows for milk, only unfortunately the latter do not give any. There are two calves. It is decided to feed them. They will probably die. In the transports special stalls have been made for the animals, so that they can endure the motion. There are none of these stalls in the battleships, and the oxen have to stand on deck.

March 7th (morning).—Our voyage is continued to the Chagos Islands, past the chief island, Diego Garcia. There were rumours that Japanese ships were lying at the Chagos archipelago, which belongs to England. The rumour may be true. Perhaps there will be a collision near these islands. The Chagos archipelago consists of small, thinly populated islands. There is no telegraph cable joining it to the mainland.

There is an artificer in the *Suvaroff* called Krimmer. He is a very trustworthy man. I once offered to exchange letters in the event of the death of one of us. To-day he handed me an envelope with the following superscription: " In the event of my death I beg you to send the enclosed letter to its address, and also to dispatch the things I leave behind. G. Krimmer, 2/3/1905. In the *Kniaz Suvaroff*." I have not prepared my letter yet. And what can I say in it ? I have no secrets from you. You know everything and what I might say to you in my last moments.

The route we are following now is little frequented by ships. Never since the creation of the world have battleships, small cruisers, torpedo-boats, or a fleet at all similar to ours gone along this route. What sort of ship is there not with us ? Battleships, cruisers, torpedo-boats, transports, a repair ship, hospital-ship, a water-carrier, and a tug.

Again the fleet has stopped. The tow-rope of one of the torpedo-boats has broken. We are going slowly. To-day at noon we have done 675 miles, in all about 1,180 versts, and we have to do 7,000 versts in order to reach the East Indian archipelago. At 4 a.m. to-morrow all warships are to coal from the transports which are with us.

March 8th.—I have been unable to write since this morning. In the first place, I was going from ship to ship; then there was such an infernal heat in my cabin that it was useless to think of writing. It is a little fresher now, 27° R. In the night the tiller rope carried away in the *Suvaroff*; the confusion was considerable, but I escaped it.

I was called early this morning, at seven o'clock. All the fleet had stopped and begun to take coal from the boats, which were loaded from the transports. At first the weather was calm, although there was a fairly large swell. The *Aurora's* steamboat disturbed me. They had hoisted it in, but I had not seen how they secured it. I wanted to see it myself. The *Roland* went about with various orders for ships that were far from the *Suvaroff*. I decided to go in her to the *Aurora*.

I went in the admiral's whaler and began to curse myself. Getting out of the whaler was very dangerous and difficult. The *Roland* had to deliver packets with orders to ten ships, and by eleven o'clock she had just been to six. The ships lay far off, and much time was spent in sending boats with the packets. At twelve o'clock I returned to the *Suvaroff* from the *Roland* in the whaler again. Could you have believed that I should ever be pulled across the ocean in a tiny cockleshell?

The swell is an extraordinary thing. It looks quite calm from a ship, but in reality it is far from being so. I drank a cup of coffee in the *Roland*.

At first she rolled lightly, but afterwards to such an extent that the plates fell from the table. When we came near the different ships they looked at us with curiosity, expected something, and asked the news, as if we were not in the same fleet. They were given the packets, and their disappointment was fearful. I was late for lunch and ate in my cabin. When I entered it from the fresh air, it seemed like a stove. The heat was intolerable. I drank water with ice in it. A piece was left. With the greatest delight I rubbed my head and neck with it. I often do this now. The ice melts instantly.

I went to the after-cabin; landed myself there on a sofa to dose a little, but it was not to be. I had begun to sleep when an orderly came and said the admiral required me. The torpedo-boat *Buistry* had dented her side slightly, broken a boat, etc. When I had finished with her I again went to the sofa in the after-cabin.

The coaling will soon be stopped. The ships are moving their engines, and we shall proceed ! It will be difficult in the swell to hoist steam and other boats on board. The weather was indifferent ; but contrary to expectation, the coaling was fairly successful. Perhaps they will begin it again to-morrow morning. The fleet does not anchor, but only lies with engines stopped. The wind and sea continually bring ships towards each other. Up to now, thank God ! everything was all right, with the exception of the *Buistry*. She ought not to have been brought. She broke up at Revel, knocked her side in at the Skaw, and now she has collided with a transport. We went on again twenty minutes ago. Dinner was late again. I have not been invited to the dining-room.

A curious impression is produced by the boxes or barrels fastened to the masts of the cruisers for the look-out men. Some of the cruisers have fastened cages, like boxes, and others have simply suspended barrels. In these boxes and barrels signalmen stand and watch the horizon.

They are hung up very high. Without them

sailors might easily fall from the mast. Only the heads and shoulders of the signalmen are visible now. A monotonous journey again stretches before us. Do you know how the officers in the wardroom amuse themselves all the evening? They make the dog listen to the gramaphone. Several pieces did not please her, and she began to howl. This employment seemed very funny to many. The gramaphone was purposely placed on deck, and the trumpet directed straight at the dog.

Nights of alarm have again begun. They suspect the near presence of Japanese cruisers, which have a base in the English Seychelles Islands, by which we are now passing.

At the wireless telegraph office they are receiving strange dispatches. There are more grounds for caution now than there ever were before. No doubt as the fleet moves forward the chances of a meeting with the enemy increase. All day I felt fairly well, but towards the evening a strange depression came over me. Anxiety wrings my heart. I have lost all interest in everything. They say that the Japanese are near. What then? It is all the same to me.

I often pass through bad moments. One grieves, rages, censures, criticises, and condemns everything. Our army is acting independently, and the fleet does not combine with the movements of the army. The self-same fleet is split into little pieces, which do not act in conformity with the movements of the others. Three (or now, perhaps, two) ships are doing something, or more probably are lying at Vladivostok. Our fleet is moving east, and the third remains behind somewhere (where we do not know); and they are collecting some remnants at Cronstadt and Libau. All these parts do not know what the others are doing. Can there be success under these conditions? I think that there are many disorders in the army. There is no method or organisation anywhere. Among our enemies all is worked out, foreseen, and guessed beforehand. They conduct war on a scientific programme. Is success likely to be on our side? No.

Of course, anything might happen. We might win, but it would only be by chance. With us it is the old system called "Perhaps," and the old game of trusting to luck. Everything is done anyhow. Not without reason some one remarked that the "apes were fighting the any-hows." To do him justice, it would be difficult to say a worse or a truer thing.

The *Oleg* is steaming astern, and other cruisers are ahead and abeam of the fleet. All the battleships, torpedo-boats, and transports occupy the centre.

March 9th (8 a.m.).—Six times to-day the tow-ropes of torpedo-boats have carried away. This is rather often. The *Dimitry Donskoi* reports that at night she saw lights of three ships, which were communicating with searchlight flashes, and were going the same course as ourselves.

Another sailor has died in the *Oslyabya*. He will be buried at sea. He died the day before yesterday, but the coaling prevented his body being committed to the deep yesterday. There are frequent deaths in the *Oslyabya*, and most of them occur when the fleet is under way.

The admiral always had weak nerves, and now especially so. He sleeps very little, is worried, and gets beside himself at every trifle. Probably he will not hold out to the end.

11 p.m.—We are going desperately slowly. So far we have made a thousand miles. If we go by one course there will be 2,800 miles left, and by another 2,500. This means we have to toss on the sea for fifteen or twenty days, if nothing happens.

At every step there are breakages and damages.

This evening the *Sissoi* damaged first her rudder and then her machinery. The tow-ropes of the torpedo-boats break like threads. The *Buistry* has again distinguished herself. She has broken a gun-platform. Soon there will be nothing to break in her.

In the wardroom they reckon that we have 4,400 miles to do in thirty-four days. Our provisions are finished, and we shall have to take to salt provisions (horrid filth). They make jokes, selecting which of the officers shall be eaten first.

To-morrow it is proposed to coal. It will be difficult to do so if the swell is as great as it was to-day. Again we shall lose a whole day. Coaling in our present condition is a very important thing, though troublesome. The whole deck is encumbered with coal, and even part of the guns.

March 10*th*.—At nine the torpedo-boat *Gromky* reported that her rudder was damaged. The divers had to work under water, and there were many sharks. While they were at work men with loaded rifles stood ready to defend them. They were clearly visible, as the water is very transparent.

9 p.m.—From a chance word I gathered that in fifteen days we shall be at some port. I doubt it,

By my reckoning we shall toss at sea much longer. Slowly, very slowly, we go on. Stoppages are constant. I am so accustomed to them that I take very little interest in knowing the reason, and am too lazy to go on deck and find out.

March 11th.—The *Svietlana* reports that she sees a steamer ahead on the same course as ourselves. It is strange that we are going slowly along an unfrequented route and yet we can catch up a steamer. Even freight-steamers do not go as slowly as our ships.

March 12th.—The *Oleg* and *Donskoi* report that they see some lights far away. They are watching them. Perhaps they are English cruisers. The steamer which the *Svietlana* saw was apparently a myth. A boiler in the *Kamchatka* is damaged, but she does not remain behind. She began to drop, but when she knew about the suspicious light she prepared to come on. We are approaching nearer and nearer to the East.

We shall soon recross the equator. Vladivostok seems like the promised land. Yes; Vladivostok, Vladivostok!

But what if my supposition about Sagalien and Vladivostok are justified? Where will our fleet go then, and what will it do? The next time we stop to coal I shall have to pass the whole day on board the *Gromky*.

They have stopped breaking the tow-ropes in the torpedo-boats. At all events, they have not broken one for some time.

The *Sissoi* is keeping back the fleet. There is always something wrong with her. This morning the *Nachimoff* joined her. The *Oleg* reports that the lights she saw yesterday were not constant. They looked like sparks flying out of funnels. Perhaps our fleet is following in the wake of some other ships. By day they hide themselves beyond the horizon, so we do not see them; and by night they approach us, having all lights out. The sparks betray their presence. At night, when there is no moon, it is absolutely dark and very difficult to see.

Our fleet is steaming with lights visible from afar; therefore it is easy for ships knowing our course to find the fleet in the ocean and to approach it without danger. We may expect any moment to be attacked at night. I cannot without horror imagine one thing—that is, that they will compel us to lie an endless number of days in some Saigon.

Then what will happen ? I calm myself with the

thought that they will not allow this, observing neutrality.

Neutrality is a fine word. It is good and convenient only for the strong. Strength is now on Japan's side, and neutrality serves her interests and is useful to her.

They say that the admiral declared that if he met a Japanese ship in neutral waters he would destroy her, remembering the capture of the *Reshitelny* (Decisive) by the Japanese. There is neutrality for you! I did not myself hear Rojdestvensky say this—but knowing his character, think him quite capable of it. However, this will not happen. The Japanese are wily. They will not separate their ships, as Russia has done. God forbid that Japan beats our fleet! The might of Russia will perish with it for ten years. The fleet will not be reconstructed for long. But if we beat the Japanese at sea and get command of it, then Japan is ruined. She will be unable to carry on war, and will not be able to feed and provide the army.

In Japan itself there will be nothing to eat. It can scarcely happen so. Even if the mastery of the sea remains with us, England and America will defend Japan, and Russia will retire, fearing war with these two countries. The war is bound to end to Russia's disadvantage. How much money she has wasted! How many men have perished!—and for what?

Shame! Shame! We wallow in shame! How we jeered at the English during their war with the Boers, at the Italians during their Abyssinian campaign! I do not know what is going on in Manchuria, but judging by the time that passed between the battles of Liao-Yang and Mukden the next great fight will take place in August or September,—in the event of the Japanese not moving beyond Mukden and acting as they have hitherto done—that is, very carefully.

By August or September Russia might collect an army.

Where is now the supply depot of our land forces? In Harbin? It may be that they will have to leave it and retire again. Yesterday I heard a quarrel among the sub-lieutenants about how many stoke-holds there were in the *Suvaroff*, and how the boilers were placed. Officers who had been in the ship a year, and who had, by order of the admiral, kept watch in the stoke-hold, were quarrelling over these things. How sad it was, and yet I could not listen to them without laughing! The Japanese doubtless know our ships better than we do ourselves. Do you remember what I said before the departure of the fleet? From the very beginning of the voyage I have seen so many instances confirming my former opinions. I do not believe in the fleet, however many ships are in it, and however much they count on them. It is a small matter to possess warships. It is necessary to profit by their strength. Possibly the Japanese fleet might be beaten, but it would only be by chance.

March 13th.—To-day is Sunday. There will be mass. I must go to church—the service is just beginning. I have not been at all well.

I slept a great deal to-day, and was punished for it. I slept in my bunk, leaving my port open. There was a fairly heavy sea. The water splashed in and poured over my feet. I took off my boots and went to sleep again in wet clothes. I woke from a second douche. A third time I was splashed over. I rose, and began to change my socks and boots. I sat at the writing-table. Another wave poured in, and literally wetted me from head to foot.

Everything on the table was drenched. I had to shut the port. Now it is so stuffy in my cabin and the air is so steamy that I cannot breathe. I am writing in the deck cabin. The weather is getting more and more rough. Perhaps it is for the best—it will be more difficult for the enemy to attack us.

By the morning we should be at Diego Garcia (one of the islands of the Chagos Archipelago), where the presence of Japanese ships is suspected. In any case, I must be prepared to go to-morrow morning to the *Gromky*, although the weather is such that it will be difficult to coal. We are going slowly. It is a good thing that a favourable current is helping us on. During the last twenty-four hours it has advanced us about fifty versts. This evening all searchlights were lit up until the moon rose.

March 14th (morning).—What a night it was!—so stuffy and hot that when I woke not only were the sheets and pillows wet, but the mat as well.

We had just done half the voyage between Madagascar and the East Indian Archipelago. We may count not only on torpedo-attacks and ground mines, but also on a fleet action.

Our voyage to Vladivostok will be very dangerous. We have to pass through straits and narrow seas. All sorts of meetings and surprises are possible. They will follow every movement of our ships, choosing a favourable time to deliver battle or make a torpedo-boat attack. Some one conceived the fancy that when the whole fleet coaled in the open sea, and lay with engines stopped, a Russian town had sprung up in the middle of the ocean, with a population of 12,000 people. If I reach Vladivostok, a distance which can be passed over in fourteen or fifteen days will separate you from me. How microscopic it will seem in comparison with what we have already passed! It will seem quite close to me.

If there are no delays anywhere, then by the middle of April the fleet will reach Vladivostok. But what is the use of guessing and calculating?—a thousand things may yet happen.

It is unfortunate that in the East Indian archipelago there are so many straits which are long and narrow. There are some which cannot be passed through in a day, and have to be traversed at night. They might be mined.

On entering or leaving them when the fleet is spread out, torpedo attacks might be made. We may expect surprises from torpedo-boats and from the shores. It is impossible to pass through a strait unperceived. I have just hit on the idea that we may possibly go to Saigon. On the way to Saigon a collison will infallibly take place. It may have sad consequences for me as well as for the others.

Perhaps I shall not be able to send letters. Let us suppose we get to Saigon. The *Diana* is lying there. She is officially disarmed. What is to prevent her joining our fleet ? Instead of the *Diana* a ship like the *Almez* might be left. That would be excellent. It would be better if we were joined by the *Cesarevitch, Askold,* and torpedo-boats. It is difficult to count on this.

All the ships are disarmed in neutral ports. It is a pity we have to pass through the straits in dark, moonless nights.

March 15*th.*—I was called at 5 a.m. in order to go on board the *Gromky.*

Divers arrived and the work began. The work is greatly hampered by the swell. The divers are constantly struck by the rudder. I am astonished at the dog's life they lead on board the torpedo-boats. Whilst steaming, the vibration is so great that it is impossible to write. They roll so much that nothing remains on the tables without fiddles (frames which support tumblers, plates, etc.). The accommodation is cramped, and it is dirty and sooty.

In addition to all this the fare is disgusting. I remained in the *Gromky* until eleven o'clock. It was time to eat, but they did not think of laying a table. They brought the crew their stchee,[1] and my appetite left me. There were only four sausages for the officers. Some officers from the *Kamchatka*, which was lying close by, were in the *Gromky*. They requested by semaphore that preserves, lemonade, etc., might be sent from her. I was so hungry that I did not hesitate to insist on their bringing sardines, ham, bacon, etc. When they arrived we all threw ourselves on these delicacies with avidity. They purposely brought more than sufficient, in order to leave the surplus for the officers of the torpedo-boat. The latter astonished me. They look upon a lack of food as inevitable. The *Irtish* should supply them with provisions, but she fulfilled the duty badly.

The captain asked that his torpedo-boat should be attached to another transport. I supported the captain's request to the utmost of my ability, and depicted in vivid colours their famished condition. Life on board a torpedo-boat is sufficiently penal, but in this one they starve as well. For the future the *Gromky* will be attached to the *Kieff*.

While I was in the *Gromky* a heavy squall went by on the beam. It was lucky it did not catch the torpedo-boat.

[1] Cabbage soup.

Several times sharks gathered near the divers, but they saw them in time and drove them away with rifle-shots. You suddenly see a large, grey, shapeless thing appearing. It is an ugly and repulsive-looking shark.

In the *Gromky* I saw friend Grishka, "the Iconoclast." This monkey has grown a great deal, and is very amusing. I think I told you about Grishka. He is the monkey who was the cause of a scandal in the *Suvaroff*, and was given to another ship. He received the nickname of the "Iconoclast," because he once stole an ikon out of the cabin and threw it overboard.

March 16*th* (evening).—Early this morning I again went to the *Gromky*. I got there with difficulty. The swell tossed the torpedo-boat all day. Heavy rain-squalls constantly flew by. The boat rolled more than 25°. Everything fell about. To sit you had to press hands and feet against something. How many times I was literally wet to the skin to-day, and got dry again, it is difficult to say. Under these conditions the divers had to work. The waves now tore them from the boat, now beat them against her, now retreating, showing the diver's heads, now hiding them somewhere in the abyss. They were rocked about under the water, and were seasick with all its consequences when in diving clothes. They had to be drawn up, as they were so faint. The work was desperately difficult. I was astonished that they went into the water again without refusing.

Picture to yourself the scene. All this was being done in a torpedo-boat in the midst of the ocean. The boat had been carried away from the fleet by the swell; we could even no longer see it. The diving-boat lay alongside the torpedo-boat. In addition to this they were coaling at the same time. It was a regular hell. The work went on very slowly.

In order to review the results of my work I sat on an outrigger (I have already told you what this is) like a bird on a twig. When rolling, the water now covered my head, now lifted me high. It was horrible, abominable, foul. It was a good thing there were no sharks.

At last, amid the chaos of waves and foam, I had to go to the *Suvaroff* in a whaler. I seized hold of a chain, pressed my feet against the side, and climbed on deck. I was wet, dirty, and could scarcely stand from fatigue. And what welcome awaited me ? A reprimand from the admiral, with a cry of " Shameful ! you serve on the staff, and cover yourself with filth. You return at five o'clock, instead of three." This is my reward! Never, never shall I forget it! True, it is my first reprimand during the seven months. What could I do? They did not send a torpedo-boat for me, as they always had done.

Nor was the *Gromky* at fault. She brought me as soon as ever she could. When the work was done she had to take the divers to the *Svietlana*, *Kamchatká*, and *Jemchug*. I was only guilty in that I was not guilty at all. Having reached my cabin, I changed my clothes, and instantly fell into a dead sleep.

There was nothing to eat in the *Gromky*, and she could not receive anything from the transport. They sent a present of a basket of provisions and a live pig from the *Svietlana*. How pleased the officers were!

March 17th (morning).—Since last evening we have been going along the equator.

We are a little to the north. How strange it seems at first! Yesterday we were in the southern half of the globe, where it was autumn; to-day we are in the northern half, where it is spring. We have missed a whole winter. There is news that the *Varyag* has been raised by the Japanese.

Possibly they have already been able to repair her, and we may meet her among the hostile ships. A pleasant encounter! Our ships will fight against us. What a disgrace!

The *Donskoi* reports that she sees occasional lights out of funnels on the horizon. That they are following us is beyond doubt. We shall go by the straits of Malacca, the length of which is about 1,000 versts. There will be surprises on going through it, and on leaving it we may count on meeting the whole of Togo's fleet. Probably among the Japanese ships will be those the Russians were unable to sink properly at Port Arthur. I have no confidence in success.

If I were in the place of the Japanese I should let the whole fleet pass without hindrance to Vladivostok, not risking my own ships in battle. It would be so easy to make a second Port Arthur out of it. A siege can be more easily undertaken there (if they have not already done so). The fortress is worse; there are less stores, workshops, and docks.

Every advantage is on Japan's side. Her success is almost sure.

March 18*th* (morning).—The weather is worse. The barometer is falling. The wind gets stronger and stronger; it has attained the force of a gale.

The *Suvaroff* inclined three degrees to the wind, and has remained in that position. My heart beats when I think of the torpedo-boats. They are being towed. I am very anxious about them. It will be dark soon. How are they faring now? They are not visible from the *Suvaroff*. The wind has gone down, but the sea is still big. The *Bodry*, one of the torpedo-boats, has her mast broken. The *Gromky* broke her tow-rope, and is going independently.

During the last coaling a steam-cutter from the *Sissoi* was sunk. All the crew were saved. The boat incautiously approached the side of a battleship, which rolled and sank her. In the *Terek* yesterday a sailor fell into the hold, and died to-day.

March 19*th* (morning).—Probably the whole world thought the fleet would go from Nosi Be to the East, round Australia or the straits of Sunda. It is proposed to go, as I have said, by the straits of Malacca. Every one will be astonished at our effrontery.

In a day or so we shall enter on a route where there are many merchant steamers. This means that in a short time all the world will know the whereabouts of our fleet and the route chosen.

At a favourable spot the Japanese may meet us

The impending battle will be one of the most momentous of the war.

Important events will soon now begin to take place. A new phase of the war which has been so unsuccessful and unfortunate for us is beginning.

We are not going to Saigon, but to Kamranh. It is a small bay, lying about 350 versts north of Saigon. On shore there is a fort and a small settlement. There is no telegraph, but apparently there is a post-office. The fleet will pass in view of Singapore.

Many officers have begun to hide their things behind the armour, in order to be able to dress themselves after the battle. I do not know whether to hide anything. We have begun to feel the proximity of the enemy. I have not yet selected the place where I shall be during the fight. Of course, during torpedo attacks one should be on deck, so that, should the ship be blown up and begin to sink, one would not have to come up from below. A ship in this event may go down almost instantaneously, like the *Petropavlosk* and the *Hatsuse*.

March 20th (morning).—Coaling has not taken place to-day. Many officers confidently rely on the fleet. They look on the four new battleships, *Suvaroff, Borodino, Alexander,* and *Orel,* as invincible.

The Japanese will put forth all their power to destroy the *Suvaroff*, in which is the admiral commanding the whole fleet. The torpedo attacks and the fire of all guns will be concentrated on the *Suvaroff*. She will be exposed to the greatest danger. It will be less dangerous in the other ships, especially in the *Borodino* and *Orel*.

The Japanese will try to kill the admiral. And what will happen then? Our ships can scarcely fly to various neutral ports and be disarmed, as has been done before.

We have been eighteen days at sea, and our port is still far away; but with each turn of the screw we are nearer and nearer our goal. It is five and a half months to-day since the fleet left Libau. Scarcely any one would have supposed that nearly six months would be necessary to get as far as the straits of Malacca.

The *Donskoi, Oleg, Orel,* and *Terek* report that they have seen lights. Hitherto the appearance of every light interested us; but now that we are near the theatre of war we regard them with complete equanimity. Is it not all the same? Would that it were sooner ended! There are people who are satisfied with the existing state of affairs.

I am surprised at them. Just now there are

officers sitting at table drunk—they are singing. Nothing like it is possible in the Japanese ships. There, they are preparing for another feast and for other songs. When shall we get our letters? Hardly before we reach Kamranh Bay.

March 21*st.*—There still remains 3,000 versts to Kamranh Bay. They say that Japanese cruisers are waiting for us there. It will be ten or twelve days' journey if nothing happens. From there to Vladivostok I think we shall go at greater speed than now, to get over 5,000 versts. They are coaling to-day.

I went to the *Bezuprechny* and *Gromky* and distributed confidential packets to the ships. Of course, I did not go to the general lunch. I lunched instead with the officer of the watch. A curious thing happened in the *Bezuprechny*. They drew a small shark out of the Kingstons. It was drawn in by the current. The ships are now forming in battle order. Probably lunch will be late. To-morrow is the new moon. It will give little light at night. It is a pity that we shall have to pass through the straits of Malacca on a dark night, when we may expect the Japanese to destroy our ships in the narrows.

March 22*nd.*—Although I did not feel tired yester-

THE REASON OF MY SLEEPINESS

day, I lay down and slept till the waves splashed in through the port and woke me.

Three sailors were scalded by steam in the *Oslyabya*; it is not yet known if they are seriously hurt. I have discovered the reason of my sleepiness yesterday. I began to smoke new French cigarettes. They had opium in them. It is a pity I have only a hundred cigarettes left. They are very dear now. I must smoke others, and keep those with opium in reserve.

The torpedo-boat *Buiny* has damaged her forward torpedo-tube by striking the *Vladimir*. Now it will not work.

The fleet will pass through the straits of Malacca in four columns. All the transports will be in the middle, the battleships on the extreme right, and the cruisers on the extreme left.

It is curious. You would expect us to be alarmed. We are almost on the eve of meeting with the enemy's fleet, with his mines, submarine boats, and torpedo-boats, and yet I am quite calm, even happy. The prospect of being at Vladivostok in a month's time is so exhilarating. I daily look at the chart with feverish interest, where the course already run is shown, and I count the remaining miles to Vladivostok.

Are they despairing in Russia and not counting

on Vladivostok being able to hold out ? If on our arrival at Kamranh we learn that it has fallen, we should then have no base. What could we do then ? We should have to occupy one of the Japanese islands and make it our base—but that would be bad for the supply of warlike provisions, ammunition, correspondence, and telegrams. They would not allow a base to be made at a neutral port. There is a report that the Japanese have made themselves at home in the islands of the Natuna Archipelago, which nominally belong to Holland. These islands lie on our course higher up, north of the strait of Singapore, which is a continuation of Malacca.

How quickly rats swim ! Two were thrown overboard to-day. They chased the ship and climbed up, although the speed was nearly seven knots.

Up to the present the newspapers have not known where the fleet is to be found. To-morrow we shall pass by the lighthouse of Pulo Way. From there the ends of the earth will be informed by telegrams.

Strange lights have appeared. Our fleet has been ordered to put out superfluous lights. Ports are covered with dead lights. We may expect an attack to-night. At last our wartime has begun.

How many restless nights are before us ? How will it all end ?

CHAPTER IX

THROUGH THE STRAITS OF MALACCA

MARCH 23rd (morning).—Yesterday the following message was received from the captain of the *Terek*: "The crew will not disperse after prayers, and demand that the first lieutenant should be changed. The latter requests to be taken off the ship's books. I consider the crew in the wrong." What? A mutiny? The last sentence is specially characteristic.

The fleet has increased speed. We are entering the straits of Malacca, and have said good-bye to the Indian Ocean. Two oceans successfully passed! What will the third bring us? The island of Pulo Way is close, but not yet visible.

During the day the shores of a small island were to be seen on the horizon, lying off the island of Sumatra. This is the first land which we have seen since leaving Nosi Be. For twenty days we have seen no land at all.

It is difficult to remain in one's cabin, owing to the heat. No other place is convenient for writing.

The ship is in darkness everywhere. This has been done purposely, in order that when the men have to rush hurriedly on deck they will be accustomed to the darkness. The battleship *Orel* delayed the speed of the fleet for two hours. One of her principal steam-pipes burst, and she could not steam. Now it is repaired. We are at present in a wide part of the straits. God forbid that a similar thing should happen in the narrows, or during the battle.

Since seven o'clock till the present moment I have been on the bridge, hesitating to go below. Nevertheless, I am satisfied—satisfied because we are moving towards the finale.

March 24th.—Yesterday we lost four hours of the twenty-four. This is bad. In order to pass through the dangerous parts by day we shall have to remain in the straits an extra day. The sooner we pass the straits of Malacca and Singapore the better.

I am surprised at myself. I am in no way disturbed. Knowing that at any moment any night we may be attacked, I continue to sleep peacefully. I go to bed undressed. I go to sleep quickly, and think little about the danger. My servant is dissatisfied. He bothers me to hide my things. He has not found a convenient place for them, and it troubles him. Though I know of a good place, I am silent. He is probably beginning a removal. I shall have to sort out my clothes, and I do not want to.

It is raining and gloomy.

This morning there were two water-spouts, but I did not see them, although I got up at seven.

The torpedo-boat *Biedovy* reported that in the morning a sailor was found lying motionless on deck. It was concluded that he was dead. They asked permission to bury him at once. The staff delayed the answer. Suddenly it was discovered that he was alive. A nice thing if they had thrown him alive into the sea!

One of the officers in the *Suvaroff* was playing with the dog yesterday. The dog grew very tired, and suddenly began to bark furiously, rushed on deck, and bit the other dogs. They poured water over it, but to no purpose. It jumped into the stern gallery, and then overboard, and was drowned. The two dogs which were bitten were tied up, as they may possibly go mad.

We have been some time in the straits of Malacca, but up to the present have not met a single steamer. At night sometimes lights are visible, and once by day smoke was seen on the horizon. It was hardly perceptible. Before the storm there is calm. It may be so now. A signal has been made that at night officers are not to sleep away from the guns they command. The crew have been sleeping at their guns for some time past. Every precaution is taken against a night attack of torpedo-boats.

We have begun to meet several steamers. They very wisely get out of their way in good time.

A heavy squall has just gone by. Until then the sea was as calm as a mirror.

The officers are distributing pots with powders for extinguishing fires, and bags containing bandages. I do not believe in fire-extinguishing powders.

The sailor about whose death there was a misunderstanding has been buried. Some one in the torpedo-boat read the appointed prayers, our priest with his cross blessed the deceased from afar, and the body was launched into the sea. How simple!

After dinner I spent three hours on the bridge with the captain. I had tea there. I asked him about Vladivostok and the life there, etc.

At noon to-day there were 2,100 more versts to Kamranh, which we can do in about seven days if there is no fight or other hindrance.

March 25th (day).—We met steamers all night, but they went aside out of our course.

The Hull incident has had its advantages. Last night we met several steamers. The searchlights were turned on them.

Admiral Enquist states that he, the captain, officers, and crew clearly saw a steamer, behind which twelve torpedo-boats were following. This can hardly be true. The Japanese are not so foolish as to show their torpedo-boats by day to an enemy's fleet. The *Isumrud* reported that she saw a steamer followed by porpoises. She hesitates to say that they are submarines, but thinks they are.

We shall soon be in a very narrow part, where the fairway is far from wide. We are obliged to go by this fairway, as it is not possible to avoid it. Something horrible may happen in it. There may be submarine boats, or ground-mines, which they may place shortly before we pass, in order that other ships should not strike them. Mines can be put down so that at a given time they will sink themselves. The steamer that is shadowing us might easily do this. She is behaving suspiciously—now going fast, now stopping, now altering course. What is to prevent her from going on ahead, and laying down ground-mines in her wake?

Even if our ships successfully evade the mines, they will in a certain period of time sink, and the straits will again be safe for neutral ships. It can all be done so simply and conveniently. Will the Japanese really allow such an opportunity to pass of damaging our fleet?

To-day there was mass. I did not go to church, but lay down. I wanted to go to sleep.

Another night, and the straits of Malacca will be behind us. The night is dark. At 4 a.m. we shall again be in a narrow fairway. We shall pass Singapore by day, and at six we shall enter the South China Sea. We shall pass the Natuna Islands, where the presence of the Japanese is suspected.

Do they intend to attack us in the straits of Malacca? By to-morrow evening this will be cleared up. Will they concentrate all their attention and their strength on the strait of Sunda, or east of it? Perhaps they do not want to undertake anything till the fleet enters the China Sea. The Japanese are enterprising. Why do they miss opportunities that are so favourable for them?

To-day we saw a long, narrow, even strip of land which was the Malay Peninsula. It is here that I again see the Asiatic Continent.

Some strange birds were flying round the ships.

They were not gulls, nor albatrosses, or any other sea-bird.

March 26th (night).—At eleven o'clock we passed the town of Malacca. The lights of the town were distinctly visible. Of course, the lights of our ships are clearly seen in the town. When we were passing it a schooner appeared on the horizon, coming towards us. The searchlights were turned on to her. A torpedo-boat approached her, and conducted her past the fleet. It was a pretty sight. Her white hull and sails showed out clearly in the darkness. She passed close to the right column of battleships.

None of the officers has gone to bed to-night. I am thinking of going now. It might happen that we shall reach Vladivostok without meeting Japanese ships. It would be a great surprise for us all. The sea is wide, and there are many ways to that port. It is possible that our extreme course will be so successfully chosen that the Japanese will leave it unwatched.

Since the battle of Mukden we have had no news of what is going on at the theatre of war. As a matter of fact, we only had agency telegrams about the Mukden fight. Many people doubt their authenticity. I believe them. Up to the present all that the French agency telegrams have informed us of has proved true.

In a few hours we shall be in the China Sea.

The officers are enumerating various reasons why the Japanese did nothing while we were in the straits of Malacca. Perhaps they have prepared for a meeting in the Rio Strait, which we shall soon pass. Perhaps the English insisted on their not causing trouble by laying mines in the straits of Malacca, where there are considerable movements of merchant ships. Perhaps the Japanese fleet is waiting for us at the Natuna Archipelago. Fighting a battle there would be more advantageous for us, because our ships could manœuvre.

We shall see if anything happens to-night. Some people suppose that peace may have concluded. If that is the case, it is a very disgraceful peace. Russia can scarcely entertain it.

I did not leave my cabin until six o'clock to-day. Going on deck, I learnt the news that the Russian consul from Singapore approached the fleet in a tug, and told us that three weeks ago the Japanese fleet at its full strength came to Singapore, accompanied by twelve transports, floating workshops, hospitals, and torpedo-boats. From Singapore they went to Borneo.

Near Borneo is the small island of Labuan. The Japanese bought land from a Russian Jew, in this island, and made themselves at home there. They connected Labuan with Singapore by a telegraph-cable. By this means they could have received news of our movements yesterday. Their fleet at Labuan consists of twenty-two warships, not counting transports, hospital-ships, workshops, and torpedo-boats.

To-night a torpedo attack, and to-morrow a battle, are almost inevitable. I must put on clean clothes, and lay in a stock of wool so as not to be deafened by the firing.

I received an extract from the log. Such nonsense is written in it that I shall have to alter it.

It is past ten o'clock, and up to now all is quiet.

The Japanese consider the 27th their lucky number. Perhaps they have postponed the battle to that date.

According to the consul the passage of our fleet through the straits of Malacca was a complete surprise to every one, including the Japanese. That accounts for our not having met with any resistance. The eyes of all were fixed in another direction.

Another ship has just met and passed the fleet. We turned searchlights on her and let her pass. At noon to-day we were about 1,500 versts from Kamranh. If there are no delays we can get there on March 30th.

Probably in this evening's telegrams is the news that our fleet has passed Singapore. We heard that Vladivostok and Harbin are still in our hands. Shall I go to bed, and if so shall I sleep? What if there is an attack? I have begun to look with equanimity on possible attacks and fights.

I do not think I shall lose my presence of mind during a battle, but shall remain calm. Soon I may put myself to the test.

Again the attention of the whole world is concentrated on the fleet. How much the war depends on its success or defeat! The hope of victory is small, but if it comes, everything will be changed at once. The faces of a good many lengthened a little when the proximity of the Japanese fleet was known. A conflict with it is unavoidable.

March 27th.—The night passed quietly. The fleet has stopped since this morning. Torpedo-boats are coaling. They had very little left, and it would not last to Kamranh. What of the Japanese? Do they not know the place where we are to

ANAMBA LEFT BEHIND

be found, and are they looking for us at sea? It is hardly likely.

Our course is clear—to the north from Singapore to Vladivostok. Perhaps they have gone ahead and are waiting somewhere. This is possible.

The question is being asked why the fleet does not go straight to Vladivostok, not calling at Kamranh. It would be easy to do this if the ships were filled up with coal for so great a distance. Coaling at sea when an attack is expected every minute is unwise and dangerous.

The torpedo-boats have filled up with coal and the fleet is proceeding. To-day there was mass. I stood thinking that perhaps this was the last service in the *Suvaroff*. Perhaps the next will be a requiem for the killed. We must expect and be prepared for everything.

7 p.m.—We have passed the island of Anamba. The admiral opines that we shall meet the Japanese fleet to-morrow. The sea is calm. There is a swell. The small ships roll. It is interesting to know what impression the news, that the fleet has passed Singapore, will produce in Petersburg. Where is the third fleet now? Will it join us at Vladivostok? Shall we await it at Kamranh? If we safely arrive at that bay, then the Japanese

will have to look after the Vladivostok cruisers, our ships, and the third fleet. They will have to divide their forces, and that would be an advantage for us. Can they not have left ships to watch Vladivostok? Is there ice there still? They say it usually breaks up at the beginning of April.

During the coming fight the *Oleg* and *Aurora* have been ordered to support the battleships that are sustaining the fight. Some of the cruisers will remain to defend the transports, which ought to try and reach Kamranh.

At noon to-day we were rather more than 1,000 versts from it, and relatively closer to our final goal. Can it be that at the very last we shall be unsuccessful? All our troubles and deprivations will have been in vain. There are too many chances on the side of Japan. It is a good thing that we passed through the straits of Malacca. The Japanese evidently did not count on our taking such a risky step. The papers, continually writing about the strait of Sunda and our colliers which were assembled there, turned their attention from the straits of Malacca. The consul, however, stated that five submarines were waiting for us the way we came. If that was the case, why did they not attack?

March 28th.—All is quiet at present. Where are the Japanese? Why have they not attacked us? Perhaps they thought they might disable some of our ships with torpedos in the strait of Sunda. The large ships would then attack our weakened fleet to decisively destroy it. The whole scheme was upset as we did not go that way. Perhaps they are now cruising somewhere near Saigon awaiting us. Our idea is to go in to Kamranh, and wait there for the third fleet and those ships which leave Russia in the spring with the *Slava* at their head.

We shall lie at Kamranh an endless number of days in inactivity, as we did at Nosi Be. We have already been twenty-six days at sea. Provisions are running short. We have taken to salt meat. At the admiral's table there is neither vodky, meat, nor coffee.

Following the general fashion, I intended to hide my things. I looked at my winter forage-cap and there it ended. I am lazy.

Our fleet has made an unusual voyage. If it succeeded in reaching Vladivostok without calling at Kamranh, the whole world would be amazed at the immensity and daring of the voyage.

10 p.m.—We have begun to receive telegraphic

signs. Possibly the Japanese cruisers are communicating with each other, seeking us.

Perhaps we shall not go to Kamranh after all. Colliers are due to arrive there on April 1st. We shall then receive our mails. This letter must be closed in good time. By my reckoning you will receive it at the end of April. By that time my fate and the fate of the fleet will be made clear.

March 29th.—South China Sea.

I sent a letter and telegram to you by the hospital-ship *Orel*, which is going to Saigon. She will be near there by dawn, if the Japanese have not attacked by that time. Then she will be obliged to take their sick and wounded, and receive orders from them. They will not sink her, as she is a Red Cross hospital. The *Suvaroff* alone managed to send letters. The other ships did not even know that she was going to Saigon to-day. An invalid officer was sent on board the *Orel*. He could not walk on board, but was hoisted up by a derrick in a special chair. A little coffee was obtained from the *Orel* for the admiral's table.

I overslept myself to-day, and only arose at nine o'clock.

It is a time of alarms. We constantly meet various steamers, principally under the English flag. The *Oleg* continually approaches to question them. This morning we met two English cruisers. One of them saluted, and the *Suvaroff* answered.

This was early. I woke up, hearing the firing. "Now," I thought, "they have begun." I looked out of my port and went to sleep again. When our signalmen first saw the English cruisers, they decided it was the *Diana* coming to join us. One of them was rather like her. Perhaps the English cruisers help the Japanese to look after our fleet. We saw seven clouds of smoke, but they quickly disappeared behind the horizon. They were evidently seven ships. A steamer flying the English flag met a detachment of our cruisers scouting, and signalled, "Have seen Japanese torpedo-boats. Beware, and look out for attacks to-night."

I am pleased that I was able to send you a letter and telegram. I do not count on receiving an answer to the latter.

The *Orel* will not stay long at Saigon. Probably you will receive my last letter in April, or in the beginning of May, when we shall be at Vladivostok, or——!

March 30th.—General coaling has been going on from early this morning. If we had continued our voyage we should have been at Kamranh about two o'clock. Now we cannot get there before to-morrow.

There is no communication between the ships. There is a great scandal in the *Alexander III*. She indicated that she had about 900 tons of coal, but in reality it proved to be only 350.

Gradually everything is coming to an end. Cigarettes and matches are scarce. I obtained a piece of soap to-day, and there is only one left.

When the coaling finished, the fleet proceeded. I did not leave the *Suvaroff*. Several times in the course of the day merchant vessels passed the fleet. I make out that we shall reach Kamranh by dawn to-morrow. We shall anchor there later.

The depth of the fairway will be sounded and searched. Although the soundings of this bay are shown on the chart, they do not trust them entirely. The search will be for fear that the Japanese have laid down mines. It will not be an unnecessary precaution. The bay has two entrances. At one of these a temporary boom will be made in order that the Japanese may not creep up to our ships that way.

10 p.m.—A sailor was buried at sea to-day. It is an extraordinary thing that it again happened in the *Oslyabya*. They have a great many deaths in that ship.

The charts with the soundings of Kamranh proved very inaccurate. One officer informed the staff that he had grounded there in some ship. The depth of the spot was shown in the chart as great, whereas in fact it was slight.

While they are sounding and searching tomorrow all the ships will coal, in order not to waste time.

Birds are flying round the ships. A heron and a dove fell from weariness near the *Suvaroff*. The heron was drowned, but the dove was rescued by a cutter loaded with coal.

The moon is now shining. In half an hour it will have set and darkness will come on. If the Japanese do not take advantage of it for a night attack, we shall be near Kamranh by morning. I am pleased. As a matter of fact, I was thrown out of my groove the moment the war began. At first there was heavy night work, I was seldom at home; then I was transferred to Cronstadt, then Revel, and Libau, and then abroad. I have had fourteen months of this unnatural and vagrant life.

CHAPTER X

THE STAY AT KAMRANH

March 31*st*.—Arrived at Kamranh. We are lying with engines stopped.

Steamboats and torpedo-boats have gone to reconnoitre and take soundings. Coaling is just beginning. As we approached this morning there was a fog. Suddenly it lifted, and between the fleet and the shore a steamer was seen. Seeing the fleet, she went full speed, hoping to escape. The *Jemchug, Isumrud,* and *Svietlana* were sent to examine her. They overtook her, questioned her, and let her go without examination.

How many steamers were allowed to go in this way! I am firmly convinced that many of them were carrying goods and provisions to Japan. We allowed them to go after merely questioning them, and not even setting foot on their decks. What sort of a fool would admit that he was taking a cargo to Japan? Steamers should be searched, and not questioned. We have let this one go. Why did she run if there was nothing contraband on board?

The Japanese would have acted differently. They would not have parted from them with answers only. Everything drops into our hands, and we neglect it. How the Japanese and their friends must jeer at us! And they are right.

It is hot here. At Vladivostok it is cold. When we arrive there the sharp change of temperature will hardly be conducive to health. There will probably be much catarrh, and even here at Kamranh it is easy to go down with the local fever. A cold wind comes from the hills.

The colliers should arrive soon, bringing the old mails. I count on receiving letters from December 13th to January 21st.

Where has that respected institution called the Naval General Staff sent our letters now? Probably they are pigeon-holed in Petersburg. We have not yet entered the bay, but are lying near it. In the depths of my heart flutters a hope that the *Orel* brings your answering telegram. The last one was a month and half ago.

We shall evidently receive nothing from Kamranh, neither provisions nor stores. It is beginning to be doubtful if we shall be able to send a mail. It is supposed that our stay here will not be long. We shall take in coal and stores, and move on.

The distance from here to Vladivostok as the crow flies, *i.e.* in a straight line, is little more than 3,000 versts. Of course, our journey will be considerably longer. I reckon that if nothing happens we can do it in fifteen days. Trying days they will be. Perhaps the course we choose will be round about, in which case we shall toss on the sea a long time.

11 p.m.—The transports and some of the torpedo-boats have entered the bay; the other torpedo-boats and warships will remain at sea, cruising round Kamranh with lights. Probably we shall go into the bay to-morrow. There are signs that we shall wait here for the third fleet. If you could but imagine what is going on ! If it were possible for me to tell you all about it, you would be amazed. Should I live, I will tell you afterwards. No, there is no use our fighting. Things have come to such a pass that I can only wring my hands and feel assured that no one can escape his fate, for this is the only possible assurance.

The weather has begun to grow cooler. The engines and boilers of all the ships are worn, especially the boilders. It is not surprising, considering that for thirty days we have not let go an anchor, Everything has its limits.

April 1st.—Kamranh Bay. We have only just begun to enter the bay, having spent thirty days at sea.

The hospital-ship *Orel* has not returned, nor have the colliers come. Have they fallen into the hands of the Japanese?

When our warships approached close to Kamranh, fishermen were seen in their boats; but for some reason not one of them came near us.

In the morning a little bird, apparently an exhausted canary, was caught on deck.

Last night was cooler. I woke up dry this morning. Such a thing has not happened to me for a very long time.

One cannot help wondering if it is wise, losing so much time at Kamranh. All the preparations Japan made for meeting us at the Sunda Straits can be transferred to another spot. They will have time to construct everything afresh. Their device at Sunda Strait having failed, it will be more advantageous for them to meet our fleet nearer their own shores, where they could at once repair their damages and where they have many bases.

All this compels me to think that we are hardly likely to meet them before passing Formosa. Of course, if we remain long at this place, circumstances may alter, and afford the Japanese the possibility of attacking us in the bay itself, and of mining it. In that case Kamranh will be an actual trap. It seems to me that the Japanese consider us more crafty than we really are. On the contrary, we are very simple. I say " simple " in order not to use a stronger term.

We have just anchored. The approaching colliers can be seen in the distance. The shores of the bay are hilly, in some places covered with growth; in others there is grey stone or sand. The sand is a curious colour; sometimes it is quite white, and sometimes yellow.

I have to go away in the steamboat. During the night, two torpedo-boats went to examine a passing steamer, and the *Blestyastchy* managed to tear the *Bezuprechny's* side. The sea is not wide enough for two Russian torpedo-boats! They must be repaired. In the *Bezuprechny* the rudder is out of order, and one engine does not work.

Officers who went into the bay in torpedo-boats yesterday state that at Kamranh there are post and telegraph offices, plenty of provisions, and that a railway is being constructed to Saigon.

A telegram was received here yesterday that the third fleet had left Jibutil. Hava's agency states that a great fight occurred between our fleet and the Japanese, near the island of Borneo. Such false news will only cause uneasiness in Russia.

Three weeks ago two Japanese cruisers arrived here, but two torpedo-boats were sent from Saigon demanding them to leave the bay. They went. Perhaps they will tell us to go away from here, and evidently it is supposed that we shall remain here a long time.

The external appearance of the bay and its entrances compare with Port Arthur. I hope it will not actually become a second Port Arthur.

They are just bringing the mail from the collier.

April 2nd.—Yesterday the admirals and captains of all ships were sent for on board the *Suvaroff*. There was a council of war.

The collier only brought from Diego Suarez letters which were addressed to Madagascar. For some ships there were no letters, and for others only two or three each. There was much swearing over it.

The hospital-ship *Orel* is approaching and brings

news. Yesterday about 3 p.m. I went to the *Bezuprechny*. The work there seemed enormous. They wanted a fortnight to do it in. I undertook to do it in forty-eight hours, and I think I shall succeed. I went to bed at four—slept in the *Kamchatka* in the captain's deck cabin. I made myself very dirty. In the torpedo-boats I always take care to wear some one else's white tunic when I have to crawl about.

I fed in the *Kamchatka*. They feed there better than in the *Suvaroff*. A Chinese cook has been engaged from Singapore for the admiral's table; perhaps the *Orel* is bringing him here.

The workmen in the *Kamchatka* are without tobacco, and pay ten copecks for a cigarette. How is this? Tobacco was sent them from the *Suvaroff*. I got on board with difficulty, as there was no boat.

At sunset I shall go to the torpedo-boat, and spend the night there. They sent off a mail while I was away. I was sorry I could not send a letter. When I leave the *Suvaroff* again I shall leave this one, and hope that it will be sent somehow.

How carelessly they deal with the post! It was decided that the *Gortchakoff* (transport) should go to Russia from Nosi Be. They sent the mail in her and many sailors' letters. The *Gortchakoff* came with us, all the correspondence is in her, and the senders think that the letters have already been received at home. It is very annoying. Several letters contained money.

The *Orel* took the invalid officer to Saigon, in order that he might go back to Russia.

When we were passing through the straits of Malacca a sailor of the *Alexander* disappeared, with his hammock. They thought he wanted to desert the ship, and had thrown himself overboard, taking with him his hammock, which was covered with cork and floats. When the *Bezuprechny* received her injury a servant thought she was sinking, and waking all the officers, he put a lifebelt into their hands.

There is a goat in that torpedo-boat. They brought her from Nosi Be. During the thirty days' passage she fed only on paper, did not eat hay, and even now refuses it. They nurse her like a baby. All the visiting-cards have been eaten by her. To-day she has been taken for a run on shore.

A boatswain and a sailor were buried to-day. They were killed by a derrick in the *Irtish*. In almost every port there are victims of accidents in the fleet.

I saw some natives—Annamese. They are of the Malay type, yellow and rather repulsive. They approached the *Kamchatka* and *Bezuprechny*, offering to sell various rubbish. The tobacco was quickly bought up, and they paid very dearly for it.

Will the *Orel* bring me an answer to my telegram? How delighted I should be if I received it!

We are coaling in the *Suvaroff*. Everywhere there is dirt and nastiness; they are heaping up coal in the wardroom and in the officers' cabins.

1 a.m.—Received your telegram. Many thanks.

April 3rd.—Transport Kamchatka, Kamranh Bay.

At last I can write. I have not been in the *Suvaroff* since yesterday. All the time I was either in the *Bezuprechny* or on board the *Kamchatka*, where I am now writing to you. I obtained paper, went into the deck-house, and am scribbling. Horrible! Whole flocks of cockroaches are running about.

The German steamer *Dagmar* weighed anchor yesterday to go to Saigon. She was stopped and given a mail from the staff. I took advantage of this, and gave my letters to be sent to her.

I am not satisfied with the work in the *Bezuprechny*. I counted on finishing it to-day, and have not succeeded. The sea and the swell hindered it. Her rudder is repaired, and they are now repairing the breach.

Yesterday a French cruiser came to Kamranh with an admiral. Salutes were exchanged. The admirals paid each other visits. To-day the cruiser left.

11 p.m.—Battleship *Kniaz Suvaroff*.

I had scarcely succeeded in writing the last page when a letter from the *Suvaroff* came for me. I found the ship horribly dirty. Everywhere there was coal-dust as thick as your finger. It hangs in the air like a fog. I do not know where or how to sleep. It is hot and dusty in the cabin. Last night I dozed, sitting on the *Kamchatka's* deck in a chair (a canvas one like those used in datchas[1]). I woke up at six o'clock in the morning.

These last days I have been feeding in the *Bezuprechny*, or sometimes in the *Kamchatka*. They feed better everywhere than in the *Suvaroff*. It has been awkward about provisions up to now. Everything has been bought up on shore. Literally nothing remains. Eggs are sold at twenty-eight copecks a-piece (about 7d.). In the morning they were selling ox-meat for nearly a gold piece.

[1] A country house or bungalow.

Altogether there are four Europeans living on shore, and forty Malays. It is almost a desert. There are only five or six houses. The engineers who are constructing the railway live on the opposite side of the bay.

There is a telegraph and post-office here. A Chinese receives the correspondence, and does it very slowly. From twelve to six yesterday he only took ten telegrams and twelve letters from two men. Twelve men were unable to hand in anything. A Chinese clerk is not a quick worker.

There is splendid sport here—elephants, tigers, monkeys, etc.

A clerk from the *Donskoi* was buried on shore to-day. Admiral Folkersham has had a stroke, but the doctors say it is very slight and not dangerous. Do you remember I told you a sailor threw himself and his hammock into the straits of Malacca? A steamer picked him up, took him to Singapore, handed him over to the Russian consul, who sent him to Saigon, and from there he was sent to the fleet. He declares that he fell overboard accidentally.

When the hospital-ship *Orel* approached Saigon she was met by a cutter and a steamer of Günsburg's, which had come to co-operate with her.

The public were not allowed on board the *Orel*. In the evening, papers came out announcing that the Japanese had been defeated by our fleet, that the *Orel* was full of wounded, whose groans were audible, although no one was allowed on board, etc. Such lies can only agitate people in Russia. The Japanese, of whom there are many in Saigon, were so offended that next day they did not leave their houses.

I was afraid I should not have been able to write to you to-day. It would have been the first time. Even on the day of the storm off the Cape of Good Hope, on December 8th, I managed to write a few words.

April 4th.—It was arranged by signal that all engineer-constructors should assemble to meet me. After having spoken to them, I set out for the *Nachimoff*. I lunched there and drank two wine-glasses of vodky, two tumblers of beer, and a little claret. It so happened that it would have been difficult to refuse them.

In the *Nachimoff* all the partitions of the officers' cabins have been broken down (so that there should not be a fire). The furniture and the sleeping-bunks have been taken away. The mattresses lie on the floor.

All the ships have prepared for battle, and present a strange appearance. Everywhere there are defences made out of chains, torpedo-nets, coal, hawsers, sailors' hammocks, etc.—anything that comes to hand. The ships have nothing in common with what one is accustomed to see.

Three elephants have been brought here for sale. It is not likely that any one will purchase them.

The French cruiser has returned, and lies in the bay by the side of our ships. It is known that a steamer will pass Kamranh soon, taking about 280 poods of rice to Japan. The admiral evidently hesitates about stopping her, fearing that he will draw on himself the accusation of making a base of a neutral port for the operations of his cruisers. The captain of the steamer is not averse to giving himself up, and will not hide or fly from pursuit.

Although we are lying at Kamranh, matters stand like this—any moment we may expect an order to weigh anchor. Everything is in readiness for this.

The sailor who threw himself into the straits of Malacca has been brought here. He belongs to the *Nachimoff*, and not the *Alexander*, as I told you before. Until the steamer picked him up he kept himself afloat in the water for nearly ten hours. To lighten himself he took everything off, only leaving a piece of neck-cover on his shoulders, so that the sun should not scorch him. He went overboard at night, and they drew him out next day. " It was trying, going on board the steamer," he said. " They all looked at me, and I had nothing on."

We have to go 4,500 versts to Vladivostok. If we do not leave here soon, we shall have dark, moonless nights.

April 5th.—Kamranh Bay. How tired I am to-day! All day long I have been going from ship to ship. They have not made me a dirk in the *Borodino*, as the officer who promised it is lying ill.

The officers in the *Oleg* are angry because Admiral Enquist is being transferred to her.

The *Aurora*'s officers went shooting, but only killed a dove. They did not go far from the shore.

April 6th.—All the battleships and the *Aurora* weighed anchor and went to sea. The rest of the ships remained in the bay.

I smoked my last Russian cigarette.

Some of the transports are going to Saigon, and perhaps will not return.

How news is fabricated! There is a Reuter's

telegram (and Reuter publishes the most trustworthy news) that in the fight with the Japanese our fleet lost the torpedo-boats *Buiny* and *Blestyastchy*, and two cruisers, the *Aurora* and the *Donskoi*. Pleasant for those to read this telegram whose nearest are in these ships. Although the cook has not arrived, the food has improved. Provisions were obtained from a steamer which arrived from Saigon.

There is a Japanese mineral water called "Jansen." A great deal of this water has been brought to the fleet. I tried it, and it was not bad.

The people who sorted the provisions behaved like wild wolves. There were some disgusting scenes. The crew of the *Orel* broke open a box and got drunk. For some reason a sailor threw himself on the doctor with raised fists, but did not succeed in hitting him. Two officers who happened to be near seized the sailor and nearly killed him. They beat his face into a pulp. It was horrible. The French saw all this, and a nice opinion they will have of the Russians.

A week before the *Orel* went to Saigon the captain of the *Borodino* ordered 4,000 eggs, hams, etc., for the crew. The crew in that ship will celebrate Easter like human beings. It will not be so in other ships.

My notebook is finished. This is the second. Can I obtain another? How much is written in these two books!—all the history of our breakages and repairs.

There is neither sight nor sound of the Japanese fleet. Will they let the third fleet join us without a fight? The *Gortchakoff*, *Jupiter*, *Kieff*, and *Kitai* went to Saigon. Cruisers escorted them. Perhaps these transports will bring us coal. There is some belonging to Russia, but will the French allow us to take it?

There are perpetual forest fires on shore. They are a beautiful sight by night. Europeans say that elephants, tigers, and panthers wander about the shore at night. The beasts feel that they are the owners. They even go up to the houses, out of which it is not safe to venture. The place is quite wild. The engineers who are making the cutting for the railway complain that the elephants cherish enmity against the telegraph-posts, and constantly tear them up. It is an interesting country, but not during such a cruise as ours.

I have not been ashore up to the present, and probably shall not go. How wearisome it all is to me! It sometimes seems that this life on board will never end. A complete apathy comes over me. Time is agonisingly long.

April 7th.—An inquiry began to-day about the sailor who attacked the officer in the *Orel*. If they look on the matter seriously, he will have to end his earthly existence.

There is a picture of the surrender of Port Arthur in the French papers. Their contempt for the Russians is growing.

They call us hares. There was one bright side in all this war—the defence of Port Arthur, and now that is besmirched.

The French cruiser is lying at Kamranh, and will remain here as long as our fleet does not leave. It looks as if she were guarding our ships from an attack by the Japanese.

Cursed war! One is ashamed to look a foreigner in the face.

Fifteen months, and not one victory! Rout after rout, and there is nothing but disgrace and humiliation.

There are several officers in the fleet who are preparing to import their wives to Vladivostok. How comparatively near that port lies! We have come a tremendous journey, and only a small bit remains. I wonder if we shall arrive there soon?

We are now waiting for the third fleet, and the Japanese are preparing to meet us. No reports about them have reached us. We do not even know where their fleet is. No doubt they know our every movement. It is all horrible. It is annoying when one sees how we do not know how to make use of our strength.

April 8th.—Our auxiliary cruisers returning from escorting the transports to Saigon met a large French steamer. There were many Russians on board her. They were in uniform, and were evidently returning from captivity. They waved their caps and cheered our cruisers.

The French admiral came on board during lunch. The meal was interrupted while he was paying a visit, which was quite unexpected. Has he come in order to request us to go ? Yes, it is so. France insists that we leave Kamranh. She is our ally, too. It is proposed that we go back 600 versts and there wait for the third fleet.

It is humiliating to go back and retreat from our final goal. If we were to wait for the third fleet, why did we leave Nosi Be ? We only give the Japanese a better chance of preparing themselves. After all, it may happen that we shall go on without waiting. Time has been lost, and our strength has not been augmented. The strength of the Japanese will be concentrated in a smaller sphere of activity, and consequently will be more effective.

In what a horrible situation the second and third fleets are now placed! Where and how shall we effect a junction?

Had it not been for the third fleet, we might have been at Vladivostok a long time ago. What will the third fleet do?

By reckonings it has only passed Colombo. From Petersburg it was ordered to go by the straits of Sunda.

April 9th.—An officer has come from the French cruiser and brought a letter for the admiral. A signal has been made to get up anchor at noon to-morrow. It is still unknown where we are going—to Vladivostok, or to some other bay. I wonder if we shall be able to send letters to-morrow? There is little hope of that, but in any case I shall be ready.

South China Sea.—At one o'clock we weighed anchor and went to sea. The transports and the *Almaz* remained in the harbour, as they were coaling from German colliers. The fleet will remain near Kamranh till they are ready and can join us. Where we shall steer then is unknown. Of course, we might toss at sea waiting for the third fleet; but coal! coal! The coaling question is the question of life.

Two of our colliers are arrested. One at Singapore and the other at Saigon. (Saigon, too, is French! How this will please you!)

Our mails have been sent to the *Tamboff*, which, after giving the fleet her load, will go to Saigon. If she does not fall into the hands of the Japanese, the letters will go to Russia.

There is an officer in the fleet who was in the *Cesarevitch* on the 28th—that is, on the day on which Witgift [1] was killed, and when our ships fled so disgracefully wherever they could. From what he says it is evident that the morale in the ships was bad, and that they were all convinced that they would return to Port Arthur; that the Japanese suffered heavily, and if our ships had held out for half an hour more the enemy's fleet would have run. He related a good deal. Obviously, we might easily have been the victors. The pity was that the spirit of despair reigned. The *Cesarevitch* hardly suffered at all. Wirenius did much harm to the fleet.

[1] A Russian admiral.

All these disgraceful stories will come to light after the war is over. Many heroes will then be taken down from their pedestals.

If we only had had clever and daring leaders the Port Arthur fleet might easily have destroyed the Japanese. What a number of mistakes we made! How little we valued our strength.

When one recalls it all one cannot account for the fatal errors. We have to pay very dearly for them. What follies they have perpetrated on land! How many young lives have been lost! How much will all this cost Russia!

The weather is becoming better. The ships are going very slowly, keeping near Kamranh Bay with lights covered. As usual, I stayed a long while on the bridge. The rainy season will begin here soon, as well as typhoons. How will the smaller vessels, like torpedo-boats, get on?

April 10th.—After lunch I am going to the *Tamboff*; she is shortly going to Saigon. I shall post this letter by her. One of the staff-officers should have gone to the *Tamboff*, but they are nearly all lying ill. I myself feel well, thank God!

Yesterday the *Oslyabya* buried another sailor.

There was mass to-day. It is Palm Sunday. How time has flown! All night the ships remained at sea. The night passed quietly. The *Isumrud* fouled her screws with a chain. Divers were sent down.

A steamer flying the Norwegian flag passed by. She was examined, but nothing suspicious was found. She was coming from Japan, and not going there.

I took my last letter and gave it to the captain of the *Tamboff*. I handed him a franc for the stamp, but he was offended and would not take it. I tried to obtain cigarettes, but was unsuccessful. The wardroom wanted to buy vodky from her, but that too was a failure. The Norwegian steamer which we examined this morning gave us the latest papers. They are all English.

The discretion of the English press is extraordinary. They consider Japan their ally, so they purposely say nothing about her fleet. About ours they print all the news they in one way or another possess. It is not the English newspapers alone that act thus. To do them justice, the Japanese carefully conceal everything, and no one ever rightly knows how many ships they have lost. Not only ships, but up to the present no one knows how many troops Japan can place in the field. It was thought about 300,000, and already they have placed nearly a million men.

The foreign press (English and French) puts our losses from the beginning of the war at about 400,000 men. If that is the case, how many are left to Linievitch? A mere trifle, about 200,000. Could anything more disgraceful than this war be imagined?

April 11th.—From time to time merchant vessels pass near the fleet. Our cruisers and torpedo-boats go and examine them. A French steamer came quite close, and a man in her expressed a wish to hand something to the admiral in person. I know now that he only announced the date the third fleet passed Colombo, and said that nothing fresh had happened in Manchuria.

A journey of only twelve or fifteen days separates us from Vladivostok. There it is cold, and here it is hot. Many of us will catch colds.

The crew are dressed badly. They have no boots, and their clothes are worn out and ragged.

The Frenchman brought no news. We received newspapers. From these it is evident that there is a great discussion about Kamranh in France. They fear the Japanese are there.

The news can scarcely be correct that Admiral Nebogatoff's fleet (third fleet) has passed Colombo. Its course is elsewhere.

WAS IT A SUBMARINE?

April 12th.—How people are deceived sometimes! It seemed to a good many in the *Suvaroff* yesterday that there was a steam cutter between her and the *Alexander III*. Instantly the fighting lanterns were uncovered, and the rays of the searchlight turned on to the suspicious place. They saw some white breakers and foam. Many are inclined to believe it was a submarine boat, disappearing under water when they began to light up. In confirmation of this supposition they point out that the *Jemchug* saw something like a periscope (a sort of tube which projects out of the water and allows objects that are above to be seen in the submerged boat).

Last evening I went to the upper deck cabin to breathe the fresh air, lay on the sofa, and went to sleep. At four o'clock I woke and went back to my cabin. I have learnt to make cigarettes fairly well. If paper and tobacco last, I can get on without ready-made ones.

They are beginning to say that in a day or two we shall leave Kamranh for another bay. To do this we shall have to take in coal and provisions, leaving the transports. The *Tamboff* apparently will not come with us. Letters will not be taken to Saigon.

A war vessel has been manœuvring in sight of the fleet. Fearing that she is Japanese, the *Oleg* has been sent to make certain. It is a false alarm. She is probably the French cruiser *Déscartes*. There is another steamer coming towards the fleet. The question of going to another bay is settled.

We are going to the bay of Van Fong, which is about one hundred versts north of Kamranh. It is probably a wild and deserted spot.

I am bored and anxious, and long to be home.

CHAPTER XI

DELAYS AT VAN FONG

APRIL 13*th*.—At about nine o'clock the signalman in an emotional voice announced that a warship was coming towards us from the north, flying the Russian naval flag and several signals. It turned out to be the French cruiser *Déscartes*. She was signalling to us, and hoisted the Russian flag so that we should understand. There is news that a hospital-ship has arrived at Batavia. It is said to be the *Kostroma*, which is with Admiral Nebogatoff's fleet.

We are approaching the anchorage of Van Fong. Some of the ships are already in the bay. The French admiral clearly sympathises with us, and if it depended on him we might lie where it is most convenient for us. He purposely shuts his eyes to a great deal. If he were not so disposed towards us it would be awkward. He is aware, for instance, where we have gone from Kamranh, but pretends that it is unknown to him. How much sometimes depends on one man!

We are moving nearer and nearer to Vladivostok. We have altogether come 28,500 versts. There are 4,200 still left. Nearly seven-eighths of our voyage is successfully accomplished.

All the ships have anchored. The *Suvaroff* is coaling from a German steamer. In the latter some of the crew are Chinamen, and perhaps there are Japanese.

I forget if I told you that two Japanese were noticed among the crew of the steamer *Dagmar*, which brought provisions to Kamranh. How well their intelligence service is organised! Wherever you look there are Japanese spies. There is authentic news that the ice at Vladivostok has dispersed. Consequently, the Japanese might undertake naval operations against it, if we do not interfere in time. It will be a fine impediment if they cut off Vladivostok by land, thus making it a second Port Arthur.

Easter will soon be here, but it is not noticed in the ship.

They live and eat as usual. There are no preparations—everywhere is dirt and coal.

April 14th.—In the torpedo-boats they were

assured that when we left Kamranh we were going to Vladivostok. They never expected we should anchor in some bay.

A sailor deserted at Kanranh. What will he do there, on that savage shore? Another threw himself into the sea from the *Rion*, having cautiously put on a life-belt. He was successfully taken out of the water and put on board the *Rion*. On what do these people count?

The shore here is hilly, and rather pretty. There is a small settlement. Chinese came near us in boats. They sold chickens, ducks, bananas, etc. The prices are heavy. They ask more than a rouble for a fowl. They will not let a small pumpkin go for less than fifty copecks.

I watched how the Chinese eat in the collier. They eat very cleverly, with sticks. It is curious to see so many people with pigtails. Sometimes they fasten them up on their necks, and sometimes hang them down their backs.

Admiral Folkersham is still unwell. He is in bed. The stroke was not so slight as the doctors said.

There are a lot of rats in my cabin. Their audacity is so great that when I sit at table they run about my feet.

The Chinese who come in junks, bringing provisions, try to get rid of false three-rouble notes made by the Japanese.

Several steamers have refused to go from the south with freights for Japan. Their captains explain that their crews do not care to go to those seas where there are Russian ships.

They tried to explain to the sailors that they themselves would lose nothing. The only risk was of losing the ship. The persuasion had no effect, so they were taken before a judge. The cause of their not wishing to continue to voyage was explained. "The Russian system," said the sailors, "is to fire at a suspicious ship and save no one. They acted thus in the North Sea. We do not want to run the risk."

Unfortunately, we do not do so; but the affair in the North Sea brought us one advantage. Merchant ships do not come near our fleet out of curiosity—they give way to us. Now steamers have no special pleasure in carrying contraband, though they can procure it freely from America. The Japanese were provided with coal long ago. The coal which we sent to Vladivostok in large quantities was captured by them.

The captain of the *Eva*, who was at Vladivostok

a comparatively short time ago, says that there is no lack of provisions there. They want matches. Perhaps he is only inventing. He also says that he has read a telegram announcing that Nebogatoff's fleet has passed Singapore. If this is true we should effect a junction with it shortly.

April 15*th.*—Last night a rat bit my foot. I must take measures against them.

At the wireless station they are receiving signals. They are rather incoherent messages. It seems as if they meant to say " Nicholas " (the *Nikolai I.* is with the third fleet). In any case, cruisers are being sent to look out for Admiral Nebogatoff's fleet.

From the *Borodino* they announce that they are getting similar signs.

An officer has just come from the *Sissoi* to report that they have received a perfectly clear message, in which the *Nicholas* asks for the situation of the *Suvaroff*. Perhaps the *Nicholas* is actually signalling. In any case, it will soon be made clear. If Nebogatoff effects a junction, then, after his ships have had a chance of being overhauled and of coaling, we shall move on to Vladivostok. Now we shall hardly wait for the *Slava* and other ships. Probably they have not yet left Russia.

There has just been a solemn service. O God!

what squalor! The crew and the choir stood barefoot. All were in white. They tried to put on clean clothes, but they were all torn. The officers' clothes were bad also. All the same, the service made a deep impression on me. It brought back to my mind the last week I spent with you.

This is the second Easter I have spent in a ship (the first in the *Apraxin* [1]), and both with Rojdestvensky.

The engineer-constructor Kostenko, who was in the battleship *Orel*, was washing his feet and somehow cut his left foot with the basin. He was sent to the hospital-ship *Orel*. He cut his tendon achilles. The flagship's doctor said he required hospital treatment. I do not yet know if his wound is dangerous. There were six engineer-constructors in the fleet. One has been sent to Russia, and one will be in hospital. Thirty-three per cent. of all the engineers have, so to speak, fallen out of the ranks. For whom else is a similar fate in store? Poor Kostenko! He is a talented man. It is not a year since he left school. Perhaps it is all for the best that he has gone to the hospital-

---

[1] In 1898 the battleship *General Admiral Apraxin* went ashore off Gothland, and Politovsky superintended the work of getting her off.

ship *Orel*. At all events, he will not have to undergo the chances of a battle.

In order not to disclose the position of the fleet, we are forbidden to send letters and telegrams from here. The question of the messages from the *Nicholas* has been cleared up. Two French ships were communicating with one another.

We have distinguished ourselves quite like Russians. We came into the bay of Van Fong, anchored, and arranged for an inspection of the entrance to the bay. The bay itself was not examined. Suddenly to-day a steamer was seen moving towards the entrance. "What is this?" "Where does she come from?" "Whose steamer?" etc. The alarm was beaten. It appears that it was a French steamer that has been lying here for four days. How this will please you! It is true the bay is very large, and there are many commodious corners in it; but, nevertheless, it does not excuse our carelessness. Why should not Japanese torpedo-boats have hidden themselves earlier, and attacked the fleet at night from the side where they were least expected. It might have happened, and they would certainly have done it if they had known that we should not have examined the bay, or that we should come here.

They say very truly that St. Nicholas the "Casual" is protecting us.

The "Apes" and the "Anyhows" are fighting indeed! I had to go and see Kostenko in the hospital-ship *Orel*. I have been only on board her once during the whole voyage, and then only because it was absolutely necessary. I am not the only one that feels like that towards her. All of us look on her with aversion, and for some reason she is not popular.

Admiral Nebogatoff, by my reckoning, can arrive on the 19th or 23rd. Several days will be necessary for his ships to repair defects, before the voyage to Vladivostok.

April 16th.—I went to the *Oleg*, had lunch there, and stayed till one o'clock. Pity it was a Lenten lunch. There was a sailor on board who had been a clown. He trained a dog and did several tricks. The cook's assistant there has received the name of "Fire King," as he eats burning tow. There are many musicians and actors there. The *Oleg* is a happy ship. The officers live in a very friendly way.

Last night I waged war with the rats for a very long time. They quite conquered. The worst of it is that they do not mind running over my bed. It is very repulsive.

I am preparing for Easter.

My servant almost by force compelled the washerman to wash a tunic and a pair of trousers for me. My shoes he has not been able to whiten.

I chatted for a long time with the navigator and captain. The latter was seated in his deck cabin without a tunic. He says it is nice like that, but it seems strange.

The wardroom are collecting creeping plants and green branches in preparation for Easter. All the same, everything is so poor and wretched. Somehow or other they have coloured the eggs, though there is no paint. The bakers have baked the bread in the shape of Easter cakes. There is, of course, no paska,[1] though there will be some at the admiral's table.

In all the Chinese boats there are eyes painted in the bows. This is done in order that the boat may see where it is going.

Those of our transports which went to Saigon have been allowed to take enough coal to last them to Odessa. Of course, if they are wise they will fill their holds as full as possible. As long as you have permission to take it, you can always gain on the amount. Do you remember in Vigo each ship was

[1] Easter puddings.

only allowed to take 400 tons, and they all took more than 800 each?

To-day, for the first time during the voyage, the agencies' telegrams have been published for the information of everybody. The captain, first lieutenant, and senior officer in the *Irtish* are drinking heavily. They are nearly always drunk. Wild scenes take place. Gloom and dissatisfaction reign in that transport. It might end very badly.

Do you know, it seems to me that the eighth will be an important date for our fleet? Perhaps a fight will take place on that date.

There are some polite wiseacres who are sending their cards to all the ships. Could anything be sillier at such a time, and under the present circumstances.

At 11.45 p.m. a service will begin, but no mass. The Easter scenes in Russia will rise up in my memory.

April 17th.—Christos Voskress![1] I woke later than usual. I am late for the hoisting of the colours. I have not yet left my cabin. Easter is being greeted. During the service half the officers and crew did not leave the loaded guns. The church

[1] Easter greeting, "Christ is risen."

was carefully covered, so that light should not penetrate outside. The stuffiness was intolerable.

The service went off with much ceremony. All were in white. The altar screen was white, and the priest's vestments also. The church was abundantly decorated with tropical plants. Everything was covered with them, and garlands were suspended from the roof. The church is so low that after it was arranged and decorated it looked almost like a cave.

We broke our fast at supper. The table was fairly well spread. No one knew in Russia that the fleet would spend Easter in the bay of Van Fong. Everything went on in the ordinary way. After 6 p.m. coal and stores were taken in, and all go about dirty.

Do you remember last Easter? It was also out of the common.

About three o'clock I went to the *Borodino*, and stayed there till six. Every officer in her received an egg and an Easter cake, and they sent eggs and cakes to the hospital-ship *Orel*. This was the only ship that did this. The others did not trouble about their sick. They promised to get me paper and tobacco.

Yesterday a mining cutter from the *Borodino*

was on guard duty, and met three Chinese boats with fish. The cutter examined them. One of the Chinamen seemed suspicious. They thought he was Japanese. He was taken into the cutter, but, profiting by a favourable moment, he jumped into the water, dived, quickly gained the shore, and ran off. A paper was found in the boat. It was apparently a simple permission for them to catch fish at Van Fong, and was written in Chinese.

I have prickly heat. It is horrible.

In the evenings, after dinner, I often go and sit on the forebridge. I was there to-day and talked with the captain. He was going about barefooted, and without a tunic.

April 18th.—The famous Meteorological Station near Shanghai gives information about a typhoon which is now on the China Sea. Will it catch us? Typhoons are very frequent. Their number depends on the time of the year. We are afraid that our torpedo-boats will not succeed in reaching Vladivostok safely, owing to them. If we go by the strait of Korea we shall have an affair with Japanese torpedo-boats and submarines. It would be a good thing if it were rather rough (like we had it in the German Ocean) when we pass through the strait. It would be more difficult for their submarines and torpedo-boats to attack us.

The last few days have been close and damp. My tobacco is mildewed. To economise in cigarettes I have to cut them in halves.

Yesterday my servant Golovko stole a bottle of brandy from the sideboard in the wardroom, and got drunk. He is no longer to be one of the servants of the staff. I shall have another. It is a pity, as I was accustomed to Golovko, and he knew my ways.

I smoked a cigarette with opium, and am now inclined to sleep. I hope Nebogatoff and his fleet will come soon. Perhaps he will bring a mail. Everything is possible with us.

April 19th.—There is a telegram that Nebogatoff passed Penang on the 15th, and not on the 13th. We may expect him here on the 21st.

There have been disorders in the battleship *Orel* about a cow. Some one broke her leg. They killed her, and gave her meat to the crew for dinner. The crew complained loudly that they were fed with meat from animals that had died.

The admiral himself went to the *Orel* this morning, and raised thunder and lightning. The captain, officers, and crew alike suffered. True, the crew of the *Orel* are a bad lot. Among the sailors are many who have been punished. Do you remember I told you they were not sailors, but convicts, in the *Orel*. Think of what has happened to this ship—her sinking, grounding, the attempt to damage both engines, etc. The captain is in a great measure responsible for the insubordination of the crew. For some reason he looks at their offences through his fingers, and even reproves the officers if they try to carry out a more severe discipline—and not only discipline, but plain order.

There is news that a French warship will arrive here to-morrow. The following comedy will be played out for appearance' sake. All the battleships, the *Oleg*, and the *Aurora* will get up anchor and go to sea at 6.30 a.m. The transports and other ships will move ahead, as if they were preparing to go. In reality they will only change their position, leaving places for Nebogatoff's fleet.

Is not all this neutrality and international right a farce? Here we have been half a month close to the theatre of war, in the waters of a neutral power. All our ships would have left Van Fong if it had not been that we feared the typhoon.

You will no doubt receive this letter when we

are at Vladivostok. It will be a pity if the letters fall into the hands of the Japanese.

I am picturing to myself the fight. An artillery fight does not appear to me to be so terrible and destructive as a torpedo attack. Projectiles could not sink a battleship or cruiser, but a torpedo might very easily, if it hit.

We weighed anchor and went to sea. On going out of Van Fong we met the French cruiser. We saluted each other. She signalled that she had some letters for us, which she will hand over to the *Almaz* in the bay. The cruiser passed into the bay, and our ships lay close to her with engines stopped. This cruiser, the *Guichen*, will leave, and then we shall return. It is a regular farce—and a farce to our advantage—that is played, thanks to the French admiral. Were it not for him the French Government would have driven us out, and there would have been an end to the business.

April 20th.—The French cruiser left, but we passed the night at sea. There is no news about Nebogatoff's fleet. It is strange. He ought to have passed Singapore, and it should have been known to us by now.

The admiral is convinced that the Japanese will try to sink Nebogatoff's ships before the latter join us. Perhaps they will not succeed in sinking them, and only damage them. They will then have to be repaired, and the voyage to Vladivostok will be put off for an indefinite period.

At eleven I heard the sound of a rocket being discharged. I put on my tunic and went on deck. Men were rushing about everywhere, hurring to the stations for battle. Shouting the question, "One or two?" They were asking about the rockets. "One" means the fleet is to exercise for general quarters; "two" means the actual alarm, when the enemy is real. There was one rocket. We frequently have general night alarms, but the men are not yet accustomed to them.

April 21*st*.—We are entering the bay. A torpedo-boat will only go to-morrow for the telegrams. That means that we can only then count on knowing something about the third fleet. For the dispatch of letters, evidently, we have to turn to the German collier. We ourselves can do nothing, like helpless children, although there is a post-office at hand.

My servant Golovko is transferred to another ship. He came to me and nearly cried. He asked me to verify my things. Of course, I did not do that.

April 22*nd*.—I have not been able to write to you

earlier to-day. I have been visiting ships. I went on board the *Irtish*. The atmosphere there is heavy. The first lieutenant is to be tried for some nonsense with the captain, by a special court. It is appointed for the 24th inst.

When I was in the *Gromky* a boat came to her in which were two adult Annamese and three boys. The boys ranged themselves in a row, folded their hands with the palms together (prayer fashion), and bowed down to their feet. I asked what they were doing. " They beg that we should buy them," was the answer. Perhaps the boys did not beg quite so much, but the traffic in children is beyond doubt. Boys, they say, are valued at five or ten francs, considerably cheaper than a pig. There were some occasions when children were bought, and they tried to make servants of them. These experiments nearly always ended badly. The boys were spoilt, and it was difficult to get rid of them.

Our captain, to whom I related the affair in the torpedo-boat, took it into his head that I wanted to buy a boy, and began to reprove me severely. With great difficulty I assured him that I did not want to buy any one. It would be a nice thing to arrive home with a ten- or twelve-year-old Chinaman !

A suspicious thing has occurred. The French admiral, whom the captain of the *Bodry* saw to-day, spoke of the movements and stations of the French men-of-war in great detail, but not a word did he mention about the torpedo-boats which ought to pass Van Fong. The *Donskoi*, which was patrolling with the *Ural*, at about two o'clock saw two torpedo-boats going north. At first they were without colours, but afterwards hoisted French. The *Donskoi* was satisfied, and did not trouble to go nearer them. The torpedo-boats passed unimpeded. The admiral and others are convinced that they were Japanese.

The rays of a searchlight are seen sometimes from the side of the open sea. It is evidently from a warship. The *Donskoi* reports that she sees the rays, and that is all. Whose can they be? If they are the *Ural's*, what is her reason for being silent? Taken in conjunction with the appearance of the torpedo-boats by day, these rays are very suspicious, even if it is the *Ural*. If she has lighted up, it means that either she has seen or suspected something wrong. The whole fleet are ordered to increase their attention. Had the *Donskoi* gone nearer to the torpedo-boats which hoisted French colours, the affair would have been clearer. If they were Japanese, how they will jeer at our foolish confidence! We saw the colours and were satisfied. As if it is difficult to hoist whichever flag you please!

April 23rd.—To-day is the Empress's name-day. We had prayers and a salute. All this time Annamese boats have been lying near our ships. You should have seen how they fled when the firing began.

Gradually everything is going. I have begun to carry tobacco for rolling cigarettes in old envelopes. It is more convenient than having it in a cigar-case.

There is no news of Nebogatoff. The officers in the *Aurora* have started a totalisator on his arrival.

The following idea is worrying me. Only vessels of less than seventy-five feet in width can enter the Vladivostok dock. I cannot say if this is true. Our new battleships (*Suvaroff, Alexander, Borodino,* and *Orel*) have a width of seventy-six feet. If it is so, in case of necessity it will be impossible to put them into dock. For some reason the width and measures of the docks are considered a secret, and do not find a place in books of naval inquiry, so that no one remembers the measures. God grant that my fears are not justified!

The duty cruiser patrolling reports that she sees three ships moving together in one direction. She is ordered at any moment to go at full speed.

April 24th.—Lights are moving near the bay. The patrol steamer signals some confused message. Can these ships be relied on? It is said that the captain of one of them does not conceal his desire to disarm. He does not conduct himself as he should under the eyes of the flagship. For instance, he is ordered to patrol three miles from the shore, and he goes out thirty. Our fleet with its necessities appears to him to be something hostile. For some reason there exists a presentiment among many that of the four new battleships the *Alexander III.* will perish during the war.

At last Nebogatoff declares himself. A torpedo-boat which went to Natrang to-day brought a telegram saying that the third fleet passed Singapore at 4 a.m. on the 22nd, and that she would join us on the 27th. Evidently all is well with it. Where has it been lingering a whole week? From Penang to Singapore is only a three days' journey. It means we shall soon leave here.

Probably my foreboding about the number eight will come to pass. I forget if I told you that it seems to me that the number eight will play a great *rôle* in the fate of our fleet.

The French admiral (Janquières), who is so friendly towards us, has sent the admiral some poetry composed by himself about Port Arthur and Stössel.

I wonder in what condition the third fleet will arrive ? What news will it bring ? Will there be any mails, and of what date ? Will it bring us tobacco, paper, and cigarettes. It left Russia more than four months after we did.

When it started we were already at Nosi Be. We have had absolutely no news from Manchuria. What is going on there ?

Janquières, the French admiral, has arrived in the *Guichen*, and has proposed that we should leave Van Fong. To-morrow we shall probably go to the bay that was examined not long ago by the *Roland*. The *Guichen* has just left. There are many in her down with fever. Owing to this the band did not play.

Thanks to all the conferences, we were late for dinner.

To-morrow the *Jemchug, Isumrud, Dnieper*, and *Rion* are going to meet the third fleet, in order to inform it of our whereabouts.

When reporting the approach of a French warship,

the captain of an auxiliary cruiser innocently asked if he should examine her. I am curious to know how he would examine a warship. There are many similar cases of sharp wit, and frequently no attention is paid to such pranks. The more I hear of the personnel and the morale in the Port Arthur fleet, the less astonished I am at its destruction, and the less pitiable it seems to me. The greatest pity is the loss of the ships.

The steamer *Eridan*, under French colours, arrived from Saigon with provisions at 9.30 a.m. I was not expecting anything, when suddenly a sailor came and handed me your letters. Apparently Günsburg sent them to Saigon under cover to his brother Mess (the real surname of the Günsburgs is Mess).

I was quite beside myself with joy. I am still more delighted at receiving news that is only a month old. At that moment the flag diving-officer came into my cabin on business. I scarcely remember what I said to him.

There were very few letters. I was the only one of the staff who received any. To-day is a red-letter day for me. I sat down to write to you, when the senior staff-officer, S——, came and proposed that I should take 1,000 cigarettes off him, out of the 4,000 he had received. They are Russian cigarettes that M. Mess sent. I am set up in smokes for a long time now.

Captain Pollis, who has recently been our secret agent in Batavia, arrived in the *Eridan*, and also Lieutenant M——, who broke out of Port Arthur in a torpedo-boat shortly before its fall. They will both remain in the fleet. The *Eridan* leaves to-day. It will be nice to send a letter by her.

April 25th.—After receiving your letters I rushed about the *Suvaroff*, and decided to go to the *Borodino*. When I arrived there the captain was asleep. They woke him. We sat down, and drank tea, and he gave me sweets. He began to plan how we should travel about Europe together after the war is over. We sat down with a tantalus and chatted. Just then they brought him letters from the *Suvaroff*. It was a pity I did not know there was a mail for him. I might have brought it with me.

It so happened that fate gladdened only two officers with news from home. In the *Suvaroff* I was the only happy one. To-day was a holiday for me indeed.

At six o'clock I went back to the *Suvaroff* in the

Borodino's mining cutter, and to my horror found that the mail had already been sent to the *Eridan*. I stuck a 5-franc stamp on to my letter. Other people gave me some of theirs, and I made up a large packet, addressing it to M. Mess. I then sent it by boat to the *Eridan*, which might at any moment get up anchor and go to Saigon.

The Annamese are queer people. They value brass and silver buttons at more than five francs each. The crew, of course, profit by this, settle their accounts with buttons, and trade in them also.

The third fleet has not yet arrived, but letters have been received for it *viâ* Günsburg. There will be a mail in it for us. I count on receiving thirty-three letters from you.

Do you remember I told you I was afraid that Günsburg's steamer *Regina* would fall into the hands of the Japanese. It seems that she was wrecked in the Mozambique Channel.

April 26th.—We did not weigh anchor in time to-day. The French cruiser came again to drive us out.

A message has been received from the *Vladimir Monomach*, which is ahead of Nebogatoff's fleet, that they are coming in complete array. We shall soon be joined by them. I am curious to know what sort of a fleet it is, what its morale is like, and what sort of captains. Many of them are laughed at. They are famous for their war service; but war changes men, and good ones are sometimes found among the bad, and *vice versa*.

2 p.m.—The smoke, masts, and funnels of Nebogatoff's fleet have appeared. Every one is in a great state of excitement, and rushes to the bridge. Binoculars are brought up on deck. At last we shall proceed. There is no need to wait longer.

When the signalling began, we asked the *Monomach* the name of her first lieutenant, to make certain that she was not a Japanese ship. She replied, and asked the *Suvaroff* the same question.

The *Dnieper*, it appears, saw the third fleet last night; but fearing that it was the Japanese, hastily retreated. She was sent in order to join herself to Nebogatoff. I am going on the bridge. The fleets are just joining. They are nearing each other. They are beginning to salute.

10 p.m.—O Lord, I do not know how to begin ! My head is completely silly. I do not know what to say. I am happy, satisfied, glad. I want to tell you everything, and am afraid shall not succeed. I shall get confused and forget.

As Nebogatoff's fleet approached we all crowded on deck. I put on my new cap for the great occasion.

First came the *Apraxin*. Could I have thought when I was working in her five years ago that I should see her here! How strange the *Apraxin*, *Ushakoff*, and *Seniavin* seemed! So short, and such long funnels! They reminded me of overgrown children with angular limbs.

At four o'clock Nebogatoff came on board the *Suvaroff*. He greeted Rojdestvensky with a kiss. The staff were invited to drink champagne to the happy union of the fleets. At table Nebogatoff spoke of his voyage and its success. His ships steamed ideally, without breakdowns. At night his fleet steamed without lights. Every one was informed about his arrival at Penang. His passage through the straits of Malacca took him two days and a half.

They brought a mail in the cutter which brought Nebogatoff from the *Nicolai I.* to the *Suvaroff*. Though it is not customary to get up from the admiral's table, I could not sit there long, and left to examine the mail. It was already sorted in heaps.

My mail had been taken to my cabin. I ran there, and did not know which to open first—

the letters or parcels. I opened the parcels. There were socks, handkerchiefs, shoulder-straps, sweets, cigarettes, soap, eau-de-Cologne, scents, brushes, etc. My eyes opened wide. My servant helped me to sort and wipe everything. It was all stuck together. How joyfully I separated all this! Indeed, I cannot say all I feel at present. I must calm myself.

The eau-de-Cologne and scents have travelled well. The jam, although it was soldered up, leaked. The cigarettes are a little spoilt, but they can be smoked. Newspapers I could not read. I only read the parts marked by you.

I am writing in broken sentences. Perhaps to-morrow I shall have to send this letter; now my head is in a whirl.

April 27th.—Perhaps the *Kostroma*, which has not joined the fleet yet, will bring another mail. You see how spoilt I am. My head is stupid to-day, but I am so pleased and happy at having received all you sent me.

I wanted to write to you, when two torpedo-boats collided—the *Grosny* and *Bezuprechny*. They must be quickly repaired. We are at sea, and the torpedo-boats are in harbour thirty versts away.

4 p.m.—I sat a long time in the whaler, waiting an opportunity to go to the *Buistry*. She took me to Port Dayot Bay, where some of the fleet are lying. I go back to the *Suvaroff* at dawn.

The fleet in general received few mails. Every one is complaining, but I am satisfied. I saw an officer in a torpedo-boat washing a tunic for himself. It was a strange sight.

April 28th.—My work in the *Bezuprechny* was successfully carried out. I returned to the fleet in the torpedo-boat *Bodry*. We met the fleet returning to Van Fong Bay to coal, as the open sea was rough.

We leave here to-morrow morning. The French sternly drive us away, but we stay on. It is impertinence. Port Dayot is really the same as Van Fong, as it is a gulf joined to it by a wide strait. It is very beautiful. The shores are hilly and covered with thick wood. In the corner of the bay lies a wrecked French gunboat, which is being dismantled. There are a lot of goats, peacocks, monkeys, elephants, and wild beasts on shore.

Yesterday I dined in the *Bezuprecnny*. The night was calm. They brought officers over from the neighbouring boats. They all live in a very friendly way. It is their custom to give each other presents on their names-days and birthdays. Sometimes the presents are very curious ones.

They invited me to spend the night, but I refused. I went to the *Kamchatka*. A cabin was ready for me there, but I preferred spending the night half-sitting in a long chair, in the fresh air on deck. At six o'clock a torpedo-boat came for me. In the *Kamchatka* they begged me to take several things to the *Suvaroff*. I did not do so.

Yesterday, in the hospital-ship *Orel*, the crew were sent into the hold for something. There were poisonous gases, and they began to suffocate. All except one escaped. The deceased was buried to-day.

The shoulder-straps you sent me are not uniform. They are an ensign's. I made a present of them to an engineer, Krimer. He was so pleased that he treated the wardroom to champagne. I did not like to give them away, but persuaded myself that I must not be a dog in the manger.

I treated some of the others to the almond cake. It smells somewhat strange, and some insects like beetles have established themselves in it.

We move on to Vladivostok the day after to-morrow. Many fear danger. After your letters I feel bold, and look to the future with hope. There is an idea that the Japanese fleet will not fight a fleet action until we arrive off Vladivostok. They will feign torpedo attacks, while in the meantime they will cut us off by land. Who can foretell the events?

For God's sake do not be anxious at not receiving letters or telegrams for a very long time. We are passing along uninhabited shores. Letters will be sent as occasions offer. Our postal arrangements are bad. Some of your letters to me are lost, and some of your October letters I have only just received.

April 29th.—We went to sea early this morning. A steamer passed close to the fleet, making an attempt to escape. Our torpedo-boats and scouting cruiser overtook her. She hoisted English colours. We only questioned, and did not examine her. She said she was going from Japan to the south, carrying coolies. We let her go.

We remain tossing on the sea. We shall leave here either to-morrow evening or day after. It is said that the hospital-ship will not join the fleet at all. Do you know, the number of ships in the fleet is now fifty-two? Some of the transports are at Saigon, or it would have been greater still.

April 30th.—The *Kostroma* has come, with a mail, it seems.

CHAPTER XII

PREPARING FOR BATTLE

May 1st.—The *Kostroma* called at Saigon and brought a mail.

The last letter I received was dated March 28th. It is quick. And all because Günsburg sent it on. All the ships have received an enormous mail. They were a long time sorting it.

To-day, May 1st, we left Port Dayot for Vladivostok. We go by the South China Sea. Our fleet now consists of fifty ships. Of these, nine are torpedo-boats, and two hospital-ships—a great armada. Probably we shall go round Formosa, and through the straits of Korea. There will hardly be a fleet action before Vladivostok. We must expect submarine boats and frantic torpedo-boat attacks.

May 2nd.—Our course is so laid that when we have passed the southern extremity of Formosa we shall go to the east of it.

At night we crossed the only course by which ships usually go from north to south. We met two steamers. They will report the course chosen by the fleet. Now we are moving in a part of the China Sea by which ships do not usually go. They are beginning to talk about coaling. They wish to arrange it to-morrow morning. The torpedo-boats are being towed by the transports. Meanwhile, there are no mishaps or breakdowns.

9 p.m.—The battleship *Orel* has delayed us for a short time. Something was damaged in her. Our course is shaped between Formosa and Luzon, one of the Philippine Islands. It is exactly seven months to-day since the fleet left Russia.

The sea is almost calm, and the ports can be kept open without danger. Hiding the lights, we are steaming with only a limited number. A collision would be difficult, as it is a bright, moonlight night. At present everything is going quietly. I rose to-day at nearly 9 a.m., was late for breakfast, and had to have it alone in my cabin.

May 4th.—To-morrow we coal—probably the last coaling at sea.

It is proposed that when the coal from the *Tamboff* and *Mercury* has been taken, they shall leave the fleet and return to Saigon. It will be possible to send letters by them.

Near Shanghai the remaining transports will leave us. Only the naval ones will remain (*Kamchatka, Irtish,* and *Anadir*), and the *Korea,* in which are war stores. If this is carried out, the admiral himself will seek a fleet action with the Japanese fleet before our arrival at Vladivostok.

10 p.m.—They are receiving signs at the telegraph (wireless) station. No one attaches any importance to them. In the ship it is surprisingly quiet. They were more perturbed when the English cruisers surrounded us in the Atlantic. I am quite composed and do not worry.

Gulls are seen; the shore is not far off. The moon is shining, and it is as bright as day. By such light it will be difficult for torpedo-boats to attack, but convenient for submarines. The sea is calm.

Soon it will not be so hot. To-morrow the sun will be at its zenith—for us, the sixth and last time.

Formosa is near. All are interested in it. With luck we shall be at Vladivostok in twelve or fifteen days.

All my preparations for battle consist in putting

my things in order. Coaling will begin at 6 a.m., if the weather permits.

At Port Dayot, not only did the transport *Gustave Lerche*, and the water-tank steamer *Count Stroganoff*, leave the fleet, but also the transport *Keenia*.

The latter is a floating workshop. Was it worth while bringing her here? She has little speed, and the workmen say is badly fitted out. I have not been there. It so happens that I have not been on board any of the ships that came with Nebogatoff.

May 5th (8 a.m.).—The fleet is coaling. The sea is calm, but the swell is so great that the battleships are rolling. It is hot. Very soon it will be cold. How shall we stand it after the tropics? There will be a large number of sick.

May 6th.—South China Sea.

Yesterday the *Tamboff* and *Mercury* went to Saigon. The mail was given to the latter. When the coaling was finished, the fleet went on full speed ahead. In the evening I drew the disposition of all ships for a lithographic stone, in the event of floating mines being observed.

It is proposed to send the *Rion, Dnieper, Kuban,* and *Terek* one after another for cruiser operations.

They decided not to send the *Ural*, as they do not trust her. It was her captain who openly boasted about disarming.

Last night I sat on the after-bridge, and waited the result of the *Oleg's* chase after a steamer. After conversing with those around I fell asleep. At one o'clock I woke, and went to sleep in my cabin. It would have been worth while waiting a little longer.

At two o'clock the *Oleg* reported that, on examination, it proved that the steamer, as the captain explained, had no documents. He himself did not know all her cargo. There was kerosene. She was going to Japan from New York. The heavily laden steamer was ordered to be brought to the fleet, was arrested as suspicious, and sent to Vladivostok for examination by the prize court. A crew of our men and petty officers were placed on board. One of them from the *Suvaroff* was appointed captain. The former captain and engineer were left in the steamer as passengers—of course, without any authority. The rest of the crew were brought to our ships.

On being questioned, they gave different evidence. Several sailors affirmed that there were guns and ammunition among the cargo. One sailor, at the very beginning, when he was out of his captain's sight, showed with his hands that there was something round in the steamer.

It was difficult to find out where the steamer came from. They all named different ports. The steamer (*Oldhamia*) will go with our crew to Vladivostok, *via* the Sungari Straits. Is this a good thing? The Japanese may chance upon her on her way. Would it not have been simpler to make certain that she carries contraband, take her crew from her, and sink her? Her capture wasted a lot of time. All the fleet lay motionless until twelve noon. She was provisioned, coaled, and the crew transferred, etc. She had very little coal, not enough to get her to Vladivostok. They began to coal her from the *Livonia*, a transport which came with Nebogatoff.

From twelve noon we went at a slow place— twelve knots. The *Livonia* is going alongside the captured steamer, to which she is made fast, and is coaling her.

How we love to make a secret of everything— not unfrequently to our disadvantage! Our staff have telegrams giving the names of the steamers going to Japan with contraband goods. These telegrams were needed to-day to see if the captured vessel was not among the ships indicated. The telegrams proved to be confidential, and had been placed in a safe, which was hidden in the event of a fight.

What is the use of telling us at all, if we, considering it confidential, do not make use of our evidence? It is astonishing! They should have published the names of steamers with contraband throughout the fleet, in order that each ship should know about them. But with us this is a "great secret." It is simply inconceivable. To conceal the names of steamers serving in the interest of Russia is sensible, but to hide from our own people the names of the friends of Japan is simply folly. It is always and everywhere thus with us.

When they were busied with the *Oldhamia* in the morning, two more steamers were perceived, one laden and the other empty. One of them was conducted to the fleet by the *Jemchug*. Of course, it was the empty one. She was under Norwegian colours, belonged to Bergen; her name was *Oscar II*. She went off to Japan. She had already served Japan for two years (some company). We let her go. She audaciously cut through the line of our ships. Perhaps she was purposely sent by Japan as a scout. She can now inform them where she saw us. She may have taken some photographs, and counted the ships. Even if she has not been sent purposely, she will nevertheless make known our position.

We have lost and wasted much time. This loss does not pay. We are wasting the bright, moonlight nights.

On the occasion of the Emperor's birthday a salute was fired, and there were prayers.

Sorting out my books, I found a clean notebook and copy-book. They came at an opportune moment, as I had finished the last.

7 p.m.—They are beginning to swear at having let the *Oscar* go without examining her.

The weather is beginning to be doubtful. Perhaps there will be a typhoon. The fleet will suffer severely.

They have just published a list of vessels which are known to be carrying contraband to Japan. Of course, the list only contains a portion of them. What have they not in them! Horses, guns, projectiles, powder, gun-cotton, explosives, blankets, milk, rails, engines, cables, iron, steel, copper, armour plates, conserves, rifles, grenades, shrapnel, wire, steam cutters, railway material. One steamer is specially fitted for raising our ships sunk at Port Arthur!

May 7th.—Pacific Ocean.

The fleet is in the Pacific. For some reason it is also called the "Great." We passed by the islands of the Batan (*sic*) group. They say there are volcanoes there. I did not see them from the ship.

The motion of the sea interfered with the coaling of the captured steamer. If the coal does not last her to Vladivostok, she is ordered to call at Korsakovsky port (in Sagalien). There are still two hundred of our men, who were coaling, on board her. Owing to the motion they could not be taken off. They will try to take them off to-morrow.

There are about 2,800 versts left to Vladivostok.

Yesterday I began to prepare for battle. My preparations were very simple. I opened a trunk, and without more ado thrust in everything—ikons, letters, and photographs of you.

May 8th.—To-morrow we are again to coal at sea. Will there soon be an end of this coaling bacchanalia? To-day we pass the Tropic of Cancer, and leave the tropics.

When I slept last night the rats began to gnaw my toes. I am heartily tired of this kind of life, with its dirt and hardships. The *Oldhamia* has left the fleet, and will go alone to Vladivostok or

Korsakovsky port, or even to Petropavlovsk, if fogs interfere. The *Kuban* was left by her, to give her a hundred tons of coal, if it is possible. The *Oldhamia* will then go on shore, and the *Kuban* will cruise about to capture contraband.

The *Oldhamia* is a new ship; her construction was only finished last year. She was occupied earlier with contraband. She took something for Japan to Dalny, and for the Russians to Vladivostok.

At first the captain of the *Oldhamia* behaved in a very off-hand manner. He jeered at us, and praised the Japanese. He did not expect we would take him from his steamer. When it was explained that he would be taken, he sang another tune, and even cried on leaving her.

The English who remained succeeded in playing a dirty trick. They opened the Kingstons in the engine-room, and the steamer began to sink. Our crew quickly found the open Kingston, and closed it. They also tore off the marks of the stocks showing where each stock goes. Our men had to find out. Yesterday, when our crew were at the boilers, there was nearly an explosion. An engineer averted the accident. Of course, the English would not have succeeded in opening the Kingston or tearing off the instructions had it not been for our folly.

It is clear as day that the English should have been followed about, and not allowed for one moment either in the engine or boiler compartments. Up to the present we have not been able to find any contraband. All the holds where forbidden cargo might lie are encumbered with a vast quantity of tins of kerosene. All the tins must be taken out to get below.

9 p.m.—About noon the *Jemchug* reported that she could see a balloon above her. Other ships also saw it. Those who saw it in the *Suvaroff* say it was like a snake in shape.

We are going past Formosa. There is no sight or sound of the Japanese.

May 9th.—Coaling did not take place. The weather was rather rough. I slept in the upper stern cabin.

The *Terek* has left the fleet, on a cruise to catch steamers.

The weather is gloomy. It is not so hot. Several men have already caught colds. Admiral Folkersham's health is bad. He will probably not reach Vladivostok alive.

9 p.m.—*North China Sea*.

We have left the Pacific and entered the North China Sea. We are going in the direction of Shanghai, where our transports were sent. It is impossible to let them go alone, now. There are Japanese ships at Shanghai, watching that our disarmed ships do not escape.

We passed by Formosa—passed by part of the small Japanese islands. Vladivostok is getting nearer and nearer. We have only to cross the North China Sea and the straits of Korea to enter the sea of Japan, on the shores of which is the long-desired Vladivostok. What are the Japanese doing? Where are they? No doubt preparing a hearty welcome for us.

There will probably be frantic torpedo attacks in the straits of Korea. The moon rises late and makes the night attacks easier. Will there be a fleet action? Probably it will be more advantageous for Japan to give battle on arrival at Vladivostok. Our fleet has made a great voyage and is bound to protect the transports. Probably Japanese mines have been placed at Vladivostok.

In seven days the whole world will be talking about our fleet. After sunset the crew are ordered to put on flannel jerseys. It is proposed to-morrow to carry out the coaling, which did not take place to-day.

Perhaps it may be possible to send letters to one of the transports going to Shanghai.

There is apparently an opportunity of sending a mail, but no one evidently is preparing to take advantage of it.

May 10th.—*North China Sea.*

The weather is gloomy, but calm, and rather cold.

The captain of the *Irtish* reports that she cannot go more than eight and a half knots. What can be done now with that transport? If she goes to Shanghai, she will have to disarm and be inactive till the end of the war, as she is under the naval flag. If she is taken with the fleet, she will be an extra burden.

I have to send off these pages myself. I can find no one wishing to send letters home. They say they will send them from Vladivostok. In the first place, will they be able to send them from Vladivostok; and secondly, it is uncertain if they get there any quicker. There are 1,200 miles, 2,100 versts, left to Vladivostok. Under favourable circumstances we shall make this passage in six or seven days.

NOTE BY MADAME POLITOVSKY

These were the last pages which were sent from Shanghai, and received by me (his wife) in the month of June.

During the battle Engineer E. S. Politovsky was below, as the battleship *Kniaz Suvaroff* had had a hole made in her, and he was probably giving instructions for its repair. The flag-captain saw him last in the sick-bay. "How are things going?" asked Politovsky. "Very badly," answered the flag-captain. Soon after this some of the staff left the battleship in the torpedo-boat *Biedovy*. Those who were below were not called. There was no need of them. They saved the "valuable" life of Admiral Rojdestvensky.

APPENDIX

TELEGRAM from Tokio, dated May 30th, to Japanese Legation (vide *Times*, June 1st, 1906).

The official statement of the Russian losses in the battle were as follows, so far as ascertained:

Prince Suvaroff   Sissoi Veliky
Alexander III.   Oslyabya } Battleships sunk.
Borodino   Navarin

Admiral Nachimoff   Vladimir Monomach } Cruisers
Dimitry Donskoi   Svietlana } sunk.

Ushakoff, coast defence   *Irtish*
Kamchatka, repair ship   Three torpedo-boats } Sunk.

Orel, battleship   *General Admiral Apraxin*
Nicolai I. „   *Admiral Seniavin* } Captured.
Biedovy, torpedo-boat

The *Almaz* reached Vladivostok; the *Oleg, Aurora,* and *Jemchug* fled to Manilla; the *Isumrud* also escaped, and some torpedo-boats.

www.ingramcontent.com/pod-product-compliance
Lightning Source LLC
Chambersburg PA
CBHW051037160426
43193CB00010B/972